W9-BRC-327

JOHN F. KENNEDY

URS SCHWARZ

JOHN F. KENNEDY

1917—1963

Bounty Books

Copyright © 1964 by Publishers C. J. Bucher Ltd.,
Lucerne and Frankfurt/M
English Edition Copyright © 1964 by Paul Hamlyn Ltd.,
This edition published 2004 by Bounty Books, a division of
Octopus Publishing Group Ltd, 2-4 Heron Quays, London E14 4JP
ISBN 0 7537 0920 1
Printed in China

John Fitzgerald Kennedy, 35th President of the United States, soldier, scholar, statesman, defender of freedom, pioneer for peace, author of hope—combining courage with reason, and combatting hate with compassion, he led the land he loved toward new frontiers of opportunity for all men and peace for all time.

From the citation on the Presidential Medal of Freedom, conferred posthumously by President Johnson at the White House on Friday, Dezember 6th, 1963.

A man of wisdom, strength and peace, he molded and moved the power of our nation in the service of a world of growing liberty and order.

PRESIDENT LYNDON B. JOHNSON

A person of broad outlook who realistically assessed the situation and tried to find ways for negotiated settlements of the international problems which now divide the world. PRIME MINISTER NIKITA KHRUSHCHEV

President Kennedy died like a soldier, under fire, for his duty and in the service of his country. PRESIDENT CHARLES DE GAULLE

He brought to the baffling problems of today a remarkable freshness of mind and flexibility of approach, and these were based upon his fundamental moral and mental integrity. THE RT. HON. HAROLD MACMILLAN

The loss to the United States and to the world is incalculable. Those who come after Mr. Kennedy must strive the more to achieve the ideals of world peace and human happiness and dignity to which his presidency was dedicated. SIR WINSTON CHURCHILL

The American people lose a truly major personality in their history and the peace-loving world a sincere champion of peace. PRESIDENT JOSIP TITO

John F. Kennedy was so contemporary a man—so involved in our world, so immersed in our times, so responsive to its challenges, so intense a participant in the great events and decisions of our day—that he seemed the very symbol of the vitality and exuberance that is the essence of life itself. AMBASSADOR ADLAI STEVENSON

...there was in the life of each of these men something that it is difficult for the printed page to capture – and yet something that has reached the homes and enriched the heritage of every citizen in every part of the land.

John F. Kennedy, Profiles in Courage, 1956

The life of John Fitzgerald Kennedy, mourned by the civilised world, was tragically cut short. His work still survives as a rare harvest for mankind. In spite of its violent end all the elements of a noble career are there in thought and deed: a sense of continuity with the past, vision into the future, dramatic elements of disappointment and triumph, stimulating glimpses of promise and fulfilment. There was ample measure in this one man's life for filling a long span of years. The beginning was so steep in its rise, so consciously aimed at coming events, that it will be potent far in the future as a determining force.

The election of every President is an event of deep significance, a notch in the history of the United States of America. The scope of a President's power is so great, no matter how he may fill his office, that he is bound to leave behind him deep individual marks upon American history – for better or for worse. It is true that the prescripted will of the Constitution, which balances each power with a counter-power to forestall any tyranny of the State, often confronts the President in his dealings with the Congress. But the fact that he stands alone, facing the 537 members of the Senate and the House of Representatives, creates a solitariness in his office of which no thinking person can fail to be poignantly aware.

The prospect of a fresh start is not necessarily bound up with the change of government when a new President comes in. Yet it is usually so when the election falls in a time of crisis and upheaval. Thus it was in 1861, when Abraham Lincoln moved into the White House. And thus it was more dramatically in 1933, when Franklin Delano Roosevelt took over the reins of government in the midst of a profound economic crisis. Again in 1953, after a 20 years' reign of the Democrats, the Republicans, with Dwight D. Eisenhower, took over at a critical time when the war in Korea had cast an anxious shadow over the country.

When in 1960 John F. Kennedy won the nomination as candidate for the Presidency and went on to beat Vice-President Richard Nixon in the election campaign, there existed neither economic crisis nor war. People in the United States seemed well satisfied with conditions. Nevertheless, both in America and the world as a whole the assumption of office by the young 35th President was seen as something of a challenge, possibly a sign of radical changes. Not least of the achievements of Kennedy was to have recognised that, contrary to outward appearance, the time had come to send out the call for a fresh start. As a born politician, he saw in this an opportunity of gaining the Presidency against the odds of an opposition which would have disheartened many other men. Yet behind his resolve there lay more than mere political inspiration. He had a conviction drawn from his obsessive study of American history, that a task had been given to his generation and, supremely amongst all his contemporaries, to himself.

So the election campaign of 1960 saw, above all, the emergence of a new generation. In his campaign, Kennedy revealed a wide range of thought. He succeeded in giving shape to the ideas and sentiments of many millions of people who had neither the gift nor the opportunity of expressing themselves. This is one of the reasons why he seemed so familiar and came so close to the young people in America and throughout the world. Inevitably his speeches and the image he presented awakened great hopes and profound apprehensions. Conservative circles, particularly the business world, proclaimed approaching disaster, economic crises, ruin of the currency, and State interference on every level. The opposition was fierce.

When John F. Kennedy went on to win his nomination and later, the election, he was young, and, outside his own State of Massachusetts, little known. He was a graduate of Harvard, highly educated, spoke in a high voice and with the quick Boston staccato. He was a Roman Catholic, and never hitherto had a Catholic been elected to the Presidency. He was a Democrat, and all the forces which by his origins he stood close to, finance and industry, were to turn against him. He lacked the tone of popular appeal, with which in politics so much may be achieved. It was precisely to those strata of the electorate on whom he most depended that his image was distant, strange, and indeed alarming. Kennedy realised, however, that it was his own generation *as such* that he had to hold on to, rather than to vested interests, or the Party machine. He had had first-hand experience of war as a naval officer. In 1943 his torpedo boat had been cut in two by a Japanese destroyer, and in this action he, although wounded himself, had saved all the members of his crew who had survived the ramming. His brother Joseph had been a bomber pilot: in 1944 he volunteered for a daring exploit in which he lost his life. To the millions of young people who had fought in the war and returned from Europe, Asia and the Pacific to rebuild their own lives, Jack Kennedy seemed close and related. It was to these younger ones that he turned. It was in the new suburbs, where the young married people lived with their growing families, that he sought and found his supporters.

He also paid heed to American traditions and did so enthusiastically and to great purpose. They are preserved in a vast fund of political literature that is carried in the school satchel of every school-child—a custom unknown in Europe. In a matter-of-fact manner, he wove into his speeches quotations from Thomas Jefferson, Abraham Lincoln or Benjamin Franklin. The surge for a new way of life which carried a nation of immigrants westwards and still lives on in America today, was reawakened by him. He applied it to the problems of the present day. Such magic words as "border" and "frontier", implying a battle-ground between civilisation and the wilderness, were offered as symbols of the fight between what has stood the test of time, and the still unmastered problems of the America of today.

Kennedy summarised all that he had said during one of the hardest "preliminaries" ever fought, at the Democratic Party Convention in Los Angeles on July 15th, 1960, when making his speech accepting the Presidential nomination: " . . . Today our concern must be with that future. For the world is changing. The old era is ending. The old ways will not do. . . . The problems are not all solved and the battles are not all won—and we stand today on the edge of a New Frontier—the frontier of the 1960's—a frontier of unknown opportunities and perils—a frontier of unfulfilled hopes and threats."

What did Kennedy mean by the unsolved problems, which had to be confronted by youthful forces? Both before and after his nomination he mentioned them over and over again. They had many facets. There was the lack of respect for America (he spoke during the Eisenhower era, when the President was prevented from visiting Japan, when the Vice-President was insulted and threatened in South America). Then there was apparent backwardness in the exploration of space and the moon, and in strategic armament. He sensed contempt for research and education, for poetry and the arts. There were deficiencies in the primary school programme, inequality and injustice in the treatment of the negro, endemic unemployment in some parts of the country, want and poverty in certain agricultural regions, slums in the great cities, and the cost, beyond the means of many, of medical treatment and care.

The bridge from the past of noble American traditions, which he constantly recalled to his audiences, and the tasks of the future which he exhorted them to shoulder—such was the typical note struck by Kennedy in his magnificent first speech as President. In the course of this Inaugural address on January 20th, 1961, he said:

"We dare not forget today that we are the heirs of that first revolution. Let the word go forth from this time and place, to friend and foe alike, that the torch has been passed to a new generation of Americans—born in this century, tempered by war, disciplined by a cold and bitter peace, proud of our ancient heritage—and unwilling to witness or permit the slow undoing of those human rights to which this nation has always been committed, and to which we are committed today."

The courage to grasp at the Presidency, whilst setting the highest demands for that office and thus for himself, was drawn by John Kennedy from three sources. One lay in the tradition of his own family and the powerful support he always found in it. He was born, the second son of the financier Joseph P. Kennedy, in a suburb of Boston. His father and mother—her maiden name was Fitzgerald—had their origins in Irish immigrant families who, living in Massachusetts, had soon plunged into the turmoil of local politics. Joseph Kennedy had already by 1917 become a wealthy entrepreneur; his interest in politics was inexhaustible. In 1932 he supported Roosevelt as a candidate for the Presidency and carried out various tasks in connection with the New Deal. In 1937 he became American Ambassador in London but resigned this post in 1940, as he was against America entering the war at the side of Great Britain.

Joseph Kennedy planned the professions and careers of each of his nine children and sought to give them the best available education and training. The eldest son had been destined for politics. His early death in the war gave John the chance, when he left the Navy, to follow his own bent towards the political arena. In this, like his father, he was uncompromising. Quick political successes gave him early confidence in his powers. He was elected to Congress at the age of 29, and at 35 to the Senate. In 150 years he was only the third Democrat to be returned by Massachusetts as Senator to Washington. He achieved the highest number of votes that a Senator from that State had ever received. The self-confidence thus gained was the second source of his strength.

The third source was his sense of American history. He seized on to this with heart and intellect. From it he derived great strength. When in 1954 he had to undergo a surgical operation made necessary by the injury to his back in the war, he used the enforced leisure to write his book *Profiles in Courage*. In this work, dedicated to his wife, he sketched the portraits of eight Senators who, during 150 years, had proved their political courage in placing the welfare of the State as they understood it, above political advantage, friendships and Party.

The book, for all its admiration for the courage of the individual, is by no means the manifesto of a young hot-head. Rather it reads as a work of political maturity. "It is not intended to justify independence for the sake of independence, obstinacy to all compromise or excessively proud and stubborn adherence to one's own personal convictions." According to Kennedy it is far more a matter of applying the individual judgment and the individual conviction within the framework of the democratic process rightly understood. He saw true democracy as an expanse of government by the people, in which the landmarks of personal conviction stood out. "The true democracy, living and growing and inspiring, puts its faith in the people—faith that the people will not simply elect men who will represent their views ably and faithfully, but also elect men who will exercise their conscientious judgment—faith that the people will not condemn those whose devotion to principle leads them to unpopular courses, but will reward courage, respect honour and ultimately recognise right."

With this book, which had a very wide circulation, the young Senator from Massachusetts in 1955 placed himself in the front rank of Senators who compelled attention. It was in that year that he seriously began thinking of Presidential office. For him this was no vague wish but a conscious and deliberate building-up of his position according to plan. His new activities now lay less within the Senate than in the country at large, where he learnt to know the electorate and the political leaders, and where he gradually made himself known to them. In the company of his brothers, his brothers-in-law, friends from Harvard and those of the war years, he systematically set about analysing the political situation in each State. Soon he had all the elements of the political play of forces assembled in his remarkable memory. At the Democratic Party Convention of 1956 in Chicago, when Adlai Stevenson was nominated as Democratic Presidential candidate, Kennedy was already so prominent that he was able to compete for the Vice-Presidency. His opponent was Senator Kefauver. The spectacular fight of the two rivals was played off before television cameras and was followed by the whole nation. Kennedy withdrew at the right moment and left it to Kefauver, together with Stevenson, to be defeated by Eisenhower and Nixon. But now he was known.

The "Primary" elections of 1960, that singular American institution, in which the prospective candidates for the highest office can test their popularity in certain States chosen by themselves, brought the first fruits of careful planning and at the same time a realisation of the obstacles that had to be cleared.

When Senator John F. Kennedy and his assistants appeared at the Party Convention in Los Angeles he had already assured so many votes for himself that the stormy propaganda of Stevenson's supporters proved ineffectual. Kennedy was nominated unanimously in the first election ballot.

As candidate for the Vice-Presidency Kennedy unhesitatingly chose his most serious rival in the fight for the nomination, the Democratic leader of the Senate, Lyndon B. Johnson. In this he showed his stature as a man and his shrewdness as a politician. At a single stroke he won over the Democratic Party machine, many influential politicians in Congress and a powerful representative of his cause in the Southern States. And Lyndon Baines Johnson was a man big and clever enough to overcome his personal disappointment, to accept the offer and thenceforward to fight for Kennedy with unconditional devotion.

During the whole election the fact that John F. Kennedy was a Roman Catholic had been recognised as a considerable obstacle. He grasped his nettle in his own characteristic way. He said on September 12th, 1960, at Houston, Texas, before a meeting of clergy of all denominations: "I believe in an America where religious intolerance will someday end—where all men and all churches are treated as equal— where every man has the same right to attend or not attend the church of his choice —where there is no Catholic vote, no anti-Catholic vote, no bloc voting of any kind—and where Catholics, Protestants and Jews, at both the lay and pastoral level, will refrain from those attitudes of disdain and division which have so often marred their works in the past."

He went on to outline the nature and function of the Presidency as he saw it—an ideal to which he was to remain true to the end: ". . . the kind of Presidency in which I believe—a great office that must neither be humbled by making it the instrument of any one religious group nor tarnished by arbitrarily withholding its occupancy from the members of any one religious group."

The Presidency of John Fitzgerald Kennedy began on January 20th, 1961, with the Inauguration speech that made even his opponents listen intently. Its tone was new and yet seemed familiar, for what was best of the quality of American tradition and American rhetoric came to life in it. As President, Kennedy lived up to what he had promised to the people. In his personality, in his writings, in his speeches made at the beginning of his term, one can recognise, looking back, a firm basis for all his decisions. It was inevitable that he should meet with bitter hostility and that in certain circles this went as far as hatred. He knew, and had often said, that this had to be reckoned with if the welfare of the Republic so demanded, according to the dictates of his best judgment and individual conscience.

Yet the clarity and single-mindedness of his actions and decisions were perceived by ever more people and ever further abroad. The integrity of his intention, his high concept of his office, of his duty and of the task that lay before America, were soon widely recognised.

Nevertheless, that did not diminish the reluctance of Congress to follow him, although both the elections of 1960 and 1962 had secured big Democratic majorities in both Houses. The alliance of the right-wing Republicans and the conservative Southern Democrats was demonstrated again and again as an obstacle standing in the way of the President's will to reform. Of the great legislative projects it was the Trade Expansion Act alone that passed into law. The Foreign Aid projects were always sharply curtailed. On the other hand, Kennedy was able to carry through his idea of a "Peace Corps", one of the happiest and most successful undertakings in the region of Aid for Development. The programme for school buildings, medical care for the aged, income tax reform, the Civil Rights Act of 1963, all remained unfulfilled.

The great decisions of the barely three years of the Presidency were only a beginning. Before they could be fully developed, before Kennedy could bring in his harvest anywhere, he was assassinated. The one sphere in which complete and tangible results were apparent was that of defence. It was decreed by Fate that in the very speech that President Kennedy had prepared for Dallas and which he was not to deliver, he would have pointed with pride to the results of the expansion (planned and carried out since 1961) of the United States armed forces. Here was a modern comprehensive defence concept for the atomic age.

In domestic policy, the most important decisions concerned the civic and human rights of the negroes, an issue which has perplexed the United States for over a hundred years. President Kennedy resolved to bring the whole weight of the Federal Government to bear on the insubordinate Governor of Mississippi, to compel him to respect the Constitution and the decision of the Supreme Court of the Union. This was an act of courage in the true Kennedy vein, for the President knew that he was thereby staking the fate of the Democratic Party and certainly his own future. It required his own special courage to lay the Civil Rights Bill before Congress and to press for its urgent acceptance, when it was plain that a national crisis was brewing and that a decisive response to the demands of the negroes could no longer be postponed. The difficulty of the decision was shown in the hesitancy with which Kennedy went to work. He had to reckon with the defection of the Southern States at a time when the election year 1964 was in view. In spite of this he made his plea for legislation that would appear revolutionary to the South and to some of the Northern States. In this he recognised that the welfare of the country as a whole called for a leadership that the President alone could provide.

On other issues he could be equally decisive. In 1962, against the warnings of the White House to practise moderation in all wage and price demands in order not to endanger the stability of the currency, the steel industry announced a rise in prices. Kennedy refused his consent sharply, indeed angrily. The industrialists had gone too far. They had, he suggested, disregarded the higher interest of the country. They had also flouted the Presidency. The Administration was attacked as "hostile to the economy". The steel industry, however, beat a retreat and announced a general reduction of prices a few months later.

The road of foreign affairs had been marked out for a long time previously, when Kennedy took over supreme responsibility. It was outlined in the Inauguration speech. To the old Allies the loyalty of a faithful friend was promised. The new States would be guaranteed their freedom, as long as they themselves took a firm stand for it. Aid to the backward territories was reaffirmed. To the sister Republics in Latin America an Alliance for Progress was offered to help them rid themselves of the shackles of poverty. To the United Nations the President confirmed his support. On the subject of tension between East and West, President Kennedy said: "To those nations who would make themselves our adversary, we offer not a pledge but a request: that both sides begin anew the quest for peace, before the dark powers of destruction unleashed by science engulf all humanity in planned or accidental self-destruction."

The first concern of this foreign policy was the Atlantic partnership. The great plan, "the grand design", was founded on the vision of a strong Western Europe, economically and politically united, of the countries of the Common Market, enlarged by the partnership of Great Britain. These countries, reinforced by an economic exchange made more compact by being based on the Trade Expansion Act, were to be linked with the great Atlantic community. The forces of disruption emanating from France proved a severe political reverse at the beginning of what was to be the last year of President Kennedy's life. The economic part of the programme, however, went on by way of the tariff negotiations in the General Agreement on Tariffs and Trade (GATT) in the so-called Kennedy Round.

What was outstanding in the 1,000 days of the Kennedy regime was the development of a new outlook towards the Communist world. Despite all the doubts and hesitations of the Allies, the President undertook the responsibility of negotiating with the Soviet Union. His first meeting with Khrushchev in Vienna in June, 1961, was an opening gambit. Kennedy's goodwill was misunderstood by the Russians and interpreted as weakness. One result was the partition of Berlin by the wall in August, 1961, a measure for which the Kennedy Administration had no ready answer. A further miscalculation occurred in the autumn of 1962. Moscow assumed that the Kennedy Government was paralysed by the impending elections and, after the indecision shown in the Cuban venture early in 1961, judged it incapable of dealing with any *démarche* in that area. So rocket bases were built in Cuba which gave the appearance of threatening the United States.

Meanwhile, however, the diplomatic and military machine of the Administration had kept pace with Kennedy's vision. He answered the challenge characteristically —with the patent resolve to allow it to come to a trial of strength, but with the restraint of one who has the advantage of superior resources and yet does not cut off his opponent's path of retreat. Khrushchev knew how to make use of the opportunity offered him to withdraw from a precarious and indeed hopeless enterprise. The solution of the Cuba crisis by President Kennedy has been described as the summit of his achievements in foreign policy. It was no summit. It was simply that the apparatus created by him and obedient to his will had by that time attained its potency. The readiness to negotiate, so often demonstrated, was shown also in connection with disarmament, and led finally to a partial success. On August 5th, 1963, the treaty for renouncing nuclear tests in outer space, in the air and under water, was signed in Moscow. Kennedy was the first to realise the limited significance of the treaty; he hailed it nevertheless with warmth as a first step, to be followed perhaps by others.

The style and method of government of President Kennedy had by then fully developed. Forming part of this method was the image that the President impressed on the people of the country. For in America power may well depend on whether the spontaneous, human, non-political comment of the masses can be won afresh every day. At the White House Kennedy surrounded himself with the brilliance that seemed to him the natural attribute of his high office. His beautiful wife, the happy family, the charming children, appeared to the people, since their comings and goings could be followed from day to day, like the pattern of near relatives. The youthful appearance of the President, in whose features nevertheless the burden of office began to be reflected, radiated assurance and self-confidence, and inspired trust.

President Kennedy, like his wife, showed plainly in their everyday life that they took literature and the arts seriously, and expected that their fellow-Americans too should take them equally seriously. It was no mere gesture that led Kennedy at his

Inauguration to request the elderly and renowned poet Robert Frost to read one of his poems, or to invite Nobel Prize winners to the White House. From countless directions he gathered in the affection of his people. How much he had gained by this was only realised on the day of his death, when the whole world mourned him. On the road to the Presidency, Kennedy had surrounded himself with men whose talents he valued, and whose loyalty was beyond any doubt. As President, he looked for talent wherever it was to be found, without regard for Party loyalty or the past record of the man he needed. Most prominent at all times was the group of his own hand-picked advisers at the White House. It was they who were best able to realise the concept of the "New Frontier". Deriving from the generation of those who saw active service in the Second World War, taken for the most part from academic or research backgrounds, they surrounded the President with that abundance of ideas and stimuli that his lively spirit needed. They gave practical form to the flights of his mind. They suggested solutions for him that were in accordance with his own wish to create a flexible, adaptable policy in domestic and foreign affairs. Final decisions, however, remained in the hands of the President. John Kennedy was conscious of the dignity and responsibility of his office, and to an uncommonly vital degree. His respect for the machinery of the State also led him to delegate decisions of importance to the heads of the Government Departments. In Dean Rusk he found a Secretary of State who brought with him a cultivated mind, world-wide experience, quietness, restraint and a knowledge of the most complex questions of administration. In the Secretary of Defence, Robert McNamara, he acquired an expert in industrial planning, someone unperturbed by prejudice and private sympathies, who was able to carry out the great military build-up and to cut out the waste in spending caused by the rivalry of Navy, Air Force and Army. For ensuring that the Federal Laws were implemented, he chose as Attorney-General his brother, Robert Kennedy.

This choice, so often ridiculed or criticised, became comprehensible when the racial problem came into the foreground of the political scene. Only an *alter ego*—a brother and a Kennedy—could carry out the will and the vision of the President with complete faithfulness.

On November 22nd, 1963, the apex of the carefully constructed pyramid was destroyed. The great promise of the fresh start of 1961, which only the spirit and will of the unusual man at the White House could redeem, remained unfulfilled. And yet, not wholly unfulfilled. For the spirit that lit the path of John Fitzgerald Kennedy during the brief term of his work in the service of the State and the people of America can never be extinguished.

The Politician

John F. Kennedy turned to politics shortly after finishing his war service in the Navy. In 1946 he was elected as a Democrat to the House of Representatives, for a constituency in Massachusetts that included his University. The youthful Congressman devoted more time to canvassing the Massachusetts electorate than to his duties in the Capitol. So while the Republican Senator for Massachusetts, Henry Cabot Lodge Jr., was campaigning for Eisenhower in the 1952 election, Kennedy captured his seat in the Senate, an important victory in the teeth of a Republican landslide.

Once in Washington as a Senator, Kennedy proceeded at first with caution, aligning himself with his Party friends from the North. It was only by degrees that the independent nature of his views came to be recognised. This occasionally landed him on the side of the men from the South, bringing him into conflict with the Trades Union representatives of the North.

In 1954 he had to undergo an operation, and during his convalescence wrote his book *Profiles of Courage*. It caused many politicians to prick up their ears, and from then on John F. Kennedy was acknowledged as one of the most promising and influential younger Senators. At the Democratic Party Convention of 1956 in Chicago he was strong enough to compete for the Vice-Presidency. Although he eventually stood down in favour of Senator Kefauver, he was by that time known from coast to coast.

In the winter of 1959, Kennedy offered himself as candidate in the seven States in which Primary elections were held. He easily

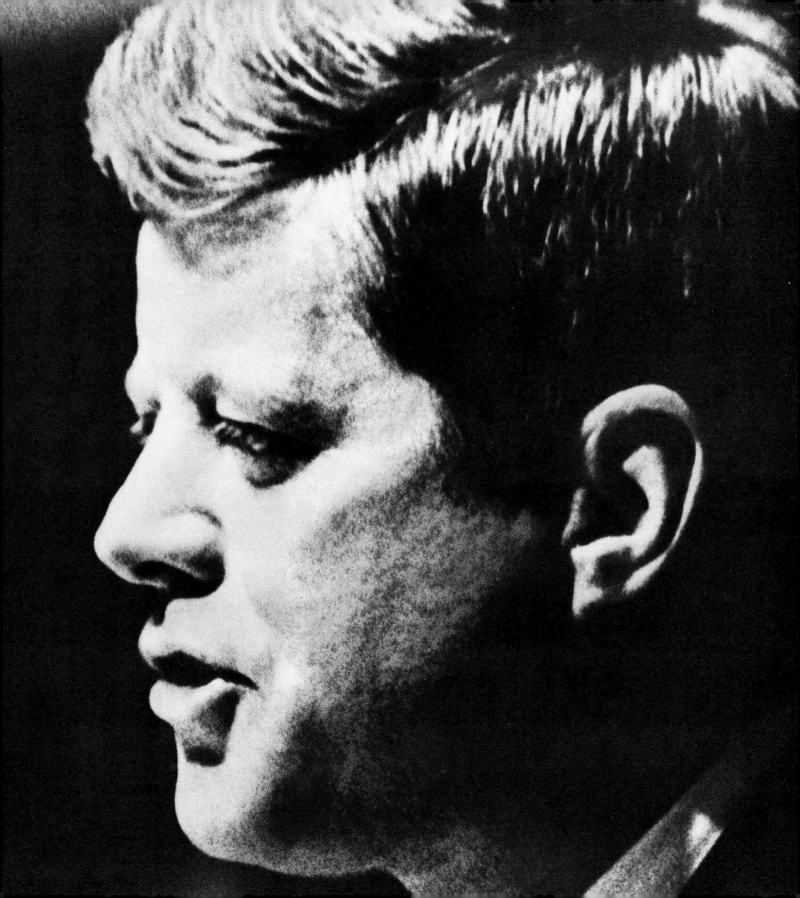

won in New Hampshire, just managed to overtake his chief rival, Senator Hubert Humphrey, in Wisconsin, and then went on to a surprising victory in West Virginia. By the time he came to Los Angeles for the Democratic Party Convention in the following July, he had already made sure of 600 votes through the Primaries and by means of long, probing conferences with Party leaders in key States.

He needed a minimum of 761 votes for nomination. He and his team proceeded to collect these votes by doggedly canvassing every single delegation, more effective, as it turned out, than the methods adopted by Adlai Stevenson's supporters, who relied on loud and sustained demonstrations on their hero's behalf at every open session. On the first ballot the Convention declared itself unanimously for Kennedy. As Vice-Presidential candidate Kennedy chose Lyndon B. Johnson, which gave him a trump card in the subsequent election.

A new element in the 1960 election campaign, in which Senator Kennedy was opposed by Vice-President Richard Nixon, was the important role played by television, and in particular the four open debates, which were given nation-wide screening. Although both candidates made telling points in the course of these debates, which were watched by an audience estimated at between 85 and 120 million people, the balance finally tilted in Kennedy's favour. His opponents' chief accusation against him had been his inexperience. Now the entire electorate realised that he had little to learn from the experienced Nixon.

Election Day was on November 8th, 1960. Kennedy gained an infinitesimal majority of 113,000 out of a total 68 million votes. 303 Electors from 23 States voted for him, as against 219 Electors from 26 States who declared for Nixon. (15 Electors and one State came out for splinter group candidates.) It was a narrow margin but it was sufficient to install John F. Kennedy in the White House.

Right: John Fitzgerald Kennedy's career as a politician began after the death of his elder brother Joseph who was killed while flying over Germany in 1944. Joseph Kennedy Jr. had been educated for a political career. After the death of his eldest son, Joseph Kennedy decided that John had to take over the mantle of leadership.

The beginning of John F. Kennedy's political career was his election to the House of Representatives in 1946. True to their family motto "Always be first, second place is already defeat", John was campaigning for a seat in the Senate in 1952. Opposing him for Senator from the State of Massachusetts was Henry Cabot Lodge Jr., son of one of Massachusetts' leading families. Kennedy's victory was substantially aided by the efforts and financial support of many members of his large and closely knit family. More and more Robert Kennedy became his brother's closest aid.

Above: By 1956 the popularity of John F. Kennedy was such that he was able to make a strong but unsuccessful bid for the Vice-Presidential nomination at the Democratic Convention. Immediately he began plans to reverse this defeat. In 1958 he decided to run for President in 1960. Once again the family became the centre of the election team. Speaking French in New Orleans and Italian and Spanish to immigrant groups in New York, the wit, charm and beauty of Kennedy's wife Jacqueline won considerable support.

At the Democratic Convention in Los Angeles in July 1960, John F. Kennedy's victory was decisive. He beat his closest rival, Lyndon Baines Johnson, on the first ballot by 806 against 409 votes and so won the Presidential nomination. To everyone's surprise he chose Lyndon Johnson as candidate for the Vice-Presidency.

In one of America's closest and most dramatic Presidential elections, Kennedy stood against the former Vice-President Richard M. Nixon. Better known than Kennedy, Nixon had the advantage of the support of ex-President Eisenhower. Kennedy's tireless campaigning, his now expert team of assistants headed by brother Bobby, his electric charm on meeting the public, and his decisive advantage over Nixon in a series of television debates, all helped him to win the Presidency.

But the New Frontier of which I speak is not a set of promises—it is a set of challenges. It sums up not what I intend to offer the American people, but what I intend to ask of them. It appeals to their pride, not their pocketbook— it holds out the promise of more sacrifice instead of more security.

The result of the election already known, John F. Kennedy, the 35th President of the United States, appeared before the press, accompanied by his wife, his parents and other members of his family. In Hyannis Port, Massachusetts, where he had awaited the election results, an enthusiastic crowd greeted him. In the armoury of the National Guard of Hyannis Port, Kennedy, in a short speech, called on Americans to support him in the difficult years to come.

One of the first visits after his election was paid to President Eisenhower who introduced him to the office which would soon be his.

Let the word go forth from this time and place, to friend and foe alike, that the torch has been passed to a new generation of Americans—born in this century, tempered by war, disciplined by a hard and bitter peace, proud of our ancient heritage—and unwilling to witness or permit the slow undoing of those human rights to which this nation has always been committed, and to which we are committed today, at home and around the world.

On January 20th, 1961, John Fitzgerald Kennedy swore the solemn oath on the Bible before the Chief Justice of the United States, Earl Warren. He then gave his famous Inauguration speech.

INAUGURAL ADDRESS, WASHINGTON D.C.

January 20th, 1961

My Fellow Citizens,

We observe today not a victory of party, but a celebration of freedom—symbolising an end as well as a beginning—signifying renewal as well as change. For I have sworn before you and Almighty God the same solemn oath our forbears prescribed nearly a century and three-quarters ago.

The world is very different now. For man holds in his mortal hands the power to abolish all forms of human poverty and to abolish all forms of human life. And yet the same revolutionary beliefs for which our forbears fought are still at issue around the globe—the belief that the rights of man come not from the generosity of the State but from the hand of God.

We dare not forget today that we are the heirs of that first revolution. Let the word go forth from this time and place, to friend and foe alike, that the torch has been passed to a new generation of Americans—born in this century, tempered by war, disciplined by a hard and bitter peace, proud of our ancient heritage—and unwilling to witness or permit the slow undoing of those human rights to which this nation has always been committed, and to which we are committed today, at home and around the world.

Let every nation know, whether it wishes us well or ill, that we shall pay any price, bear any burden, meet any hardship, support any friend or oppose any foe to assure the survival and success of liberty.

This much we pledge—and more.

To those old Allies whose cultural and spiritual origins we share, we pledge the loyalty of faithful friends. United, there is little we cannot do in a host of co-operative ventures. Divided, there is little we can do—for we dare not meet a powerful challenge at odds and split asunder.

To those new States whom we welcome to the ranks of the free, we pledge our word that one form of colonial control shall not have passed away merely to be replaced by a far more iron tyranny. We shall not always expect to find them supporting our view. But we shall always hope to find them strongly supporting their own freedom—and to remember that, in the past, those who foolishly sought power by riding the back of the tiger ended up inside.

To those people in the huts and villages of half the globe struggling to break the bonds of mass misery, we pledge our best efforts to help them help themselves, for whatever period is required—not because the Communists may be doing it, not because we seek their votes, but because it is right. If a free society cannot help the many who are poor, it cannot save the few who are rich.

To our sister republics, south of our border, we offer a special pledge—to convert our good words into good deeds—in a new alliance for progress—to assist free men and free governments in casting off the chains of poverty. But this peaceful revolution of hope cannot become the prey of hostile powers. Let all our neighbours know that we shall join with them to oppose aggression or subversion anywhere in the Americas. And let every other power know that this hemisphere intends to remain the master of its own house.

To that world assembly of sovereign States, the United Nations, (our last best hope in an age where the instruments of war have far outpaced the instruments of peace) we renew our pledge of support—to prevent it from becoming merely a forum for invective—to strengthen its shield of the new and the weak—and to enlarge the area in which its writ may run.

Finally, to those nations who would make themselves our adversary, we offer not a pledge but a request: that both sides begin anew the quest for peace, before the dark powers of destruction unleashed by science engulf all humanity in planned or accidental self-destruction.

We dare not tempt them with weakness. For only when our arms are sufficient beyond doubt can we be certain beyond doubt that they will never be employed.

But neither can two great and powerful groups of nations take comfort from our present course—both sides overburdened by the cost of modern weapons, both rightly alarmed by the steady spread of the deadly atom, yet both racing to alter that uncertain balance of terror that stays the hand of mankind's final war.

So let us begin anew—remembering on both sides that civility is not a sign of weakness, and sincerity is always subject to proof. Let us never negotiate out of fear. But let us never fear to negotiate.

Let both sides explore what problems unite us instead of belabouring those problems that divide us.

Let both sides, for the first time, formulate serious and precise proposals for the inspection and control of arms—and bring the absolute power to destroy other nations under the absolute control of all nations.

Let both sides seek to invoke the wonders of science instead of its terrors. Together let us explore the stars, conquer the deserts, eradicate disease, tap the ocean depths and encourage the arts and commerce.

Let both sides unite to heed in all corners of the earth the command of Isaiah—to "undo the heavy burdens . . . (and) let the oppressed go free."

And if a beach-head of co-operation may push back the jungle of suspicion, let both sides join in creating a new endeavour, not a new balance of power, but a new world of law, where the strong are just and the weak secure and the peace preserved.

All this will not be finished in the first one hundred days. Nor will it be finished in the first one thousand days, nor in the life of this Administration, nor even perhaps in our lifetime on this planet. But let us begin.

In your hands, my fellow citizens, more than mine, will rest the final success or failure of our course. Since this country was founded, each generation of Americans has been summoned to give testimony to its national loyalty. The graves of young Americans who answered the call to service surround the globe.

Now the trumpet summons us again—not as a call to bear arms, though arms we need—not as a call to battle, though embattled we are—but a call to bear the burden of a long twilight struggle, year in and year out, "rejoicing in hope, patient in tribulation"—a struggle against the common enemies of man: tyranny, poverty, disease and war itself.

Can we forge against these enemies a grand and global alliance, north and south, east and west, that can assure a more fruitful life for all mankind? Will you join in that historic effort?

In the long history of the world, only a few generations have been granted the role of defending freedom in its hour of maximum danger. I do not shrink from this responsibility—I welcome it. I do not believe that any of us would exchange places with any other people or any other generation. The energy, the faith, the devotion which we bring to this endeavour will light our country and all who serve it—and the glow from that fire can truly light the world.

And so, my fellow Americans, ask not what your country can do for you—ask what you can do for your country.

My fellow citizens of the world: ask not what America will do for you, but what together we can do for the freedom of man.

Finally, whether you are citizens of America or citizens of the world, ask of us here the same high standards of strength and sacrifice which we ask of you. With a good conscience our only sure reward, with history the final judge of our deeds, let us go forth to lead the land we love, asking His blessing and His help, but knowing that here on earth God's work must truly be our own.

FROM PRESIDENT KENNEDY'S STATE OF THE UNION MESSAGE TO THE U.S. CONGRESS

January 30th, 1961

It is a pleasure to return from whence I came. You are my oldest friends in Washington—and this House is my oldest home. It was here, more than fourteen years ago, that I first took the oath of federal office. It was here, for fourteen years, that I gained both knowledge and inspiration from members of both parties in both Houses—from your wise and generous leaders—and from the pronouncements which I can vividly recall, sitting where you now sit—including the programmes of two great Presidents, the un-dimmed eloquence of Churchill, the soaring idealism of Nehru, the steadfast words of de Gaulle. To speak from this same historic rostrum is a sobering experience. To be back among so many friends is a happy one.

I am confident that friendship will continue. Our Constitution wisely assigns both joint and separate roles to each branch of the Government; and a President and Congress who hold each other in mutual respect will neither permit nor attempt any trespass. For my part, I shall withhold from neither the Congress nor the people any fact or report, past, present or future, which is necessary for an informed judgment of our conduct and hazards. I shall neither shift the burden of executive decisions to the Congress, nor avoid responsibility for the outcome of those decisions.

I speak today in an hour of national peril and national opportunity. Before my term has ended, we shall have to test anew whether a nation organised and governed such as ours can endure. The outcome is by no means certain. The answers are by no means clear. All of us together—this

Administration, this Congress, this nation—must forge those answers.

But today, were I to offer—after little more than a week in office— detailed legislation to remedy every national ill, the Congress would rightly wonder whether the desire for speed had replaced the duty of responsibility.

The present state of our economy is disturbing. We take office in the wake of seven months of recession, three-and-a-half years of slack, seven years of diminished economic growth, and nine years of falling farm income.

Business bankruptcies have reached their highest level since the great depression. Since 1951 farm income has been squeezed down by 25 per cent. Save for a brief period in 1958, insured unemployment is at the highest peak in our history. Of some five-and-a-half million Americans without jobs, more than one million have been searching for work for more than four months. And during each month some 150,000 workers are exhausting their already meagre jobless benefit rights.

Nearly one-eighth of those who are without jobs live almost without hope in nearly one hundred especially depressed and troubled areas. The rest include new school graduates unable to use their talents, farmers forced to give up the part-time jobs that balanced their budgets, skilled and unskilled workers laid off in such important industries as metals, machinery, automobiles and apparel.

Our recovery from the 1958 recession, moreover, was anaemic and incomplete.

In short, the American economy is in trouble. The most resourceful industrialised country on earth ranks among the last in economic growth. Since last spring our economic growth rate has actually receded. Business investment is in a decline. Profits have fallen below predicted levels. Construction is off. A million unsold automobiles are in inventory. Fewer people are working—and the average work week has shrunk well below 40 hours. Yet prices have continued to rise.

Economic prophecy is at best an uncertain art—as demonstrated by the prediction one year ago from this same podium that 1960 would be "the most prosperous year in our history". Nevertheless, forecasts of continued slack and only slightly reduced unemployment through 1961 and 1962 have been made with alarming unanimity—and this Administration does not intend to stand helplessly by.

We cannot afford to waste idle hours and empty plants while awaiting the end of a recession. We must show the world what a free economy can do—to reduce unemployment, to put unused capacity to work, to spur new productivity, and to foster high economic growth within a range of sound fiscal policies and relative price stability.

Efficient expansion at home, stimulating the new plant and technology that can make our goods more competitive, is also the key to the international balance of payments problem. Laying aside all alarmist talk and panicky solutions, let us put that knotty problem in its proper perspective.

It is true that, since 1958, the gap between the dollars we spend or invest abroad and the dollars returned to us has substantially widened. This overall deficit in our balance of payments increased by nearly $11 billion in the last three years—and holders of dollars abroad converted them to gold in such quantity as to cause a total outflow of nearly $5 billion of gold from our reserves. The 1959 deficit was caused in large part by the failure of our exports to penetrate foreign markets—the result both of restrictions on our goods and our own uncompetitive prices. The 1960 deficit, on the other hand, was more the result of an increase in private capital outflow seeking new opportunity, higher return or speculative advantage abroad.

Meanwhile this country has continued to bear more than its share of the West's military and foreign aid obligations. Under existing policies, another deficit of $2 billion is predicted for 1961—and individuals in those countries whose dollar position once depended on these deficits for improvement now wonder aloud whether our gold reserves will remain sufficient to meet our own obligations.

All this is cause for concern—but it is not cause for panic. For our monetary and financial position remains exceedingly strong. Including our drawing rights in the International Monetary Fund and the gold reserve held as backing for our currency and Federal Reserve deposits, we have some $22 billion in total gold stocks and other international monetary reserves—and I now pledge that their full strength stands behind the value of the dollar for use if needed.

Moreover, we hold large assets abroad—the total owed this nation far exceeds the claims upon our reserves—and our exports once again substantially exceed our imports.

In short, we need not—and we shall not—take any action to increase the dollar price of gold from $35 an ounce—to impose exchange controls—to reduce our anti-recession efforts—to fall back on restrictive trade policies—or to weaken our commitments around the world.

This Administration will not distort the value of the dollar in any fashion. And this is a commitment.

Prudence and good sense do require, however, that new steps be taken to ease the payments deficit and prevent any gold crisis. Our success in world affairs has long depended in part upon foreign confidence in our ability to pay. A series of executive orders, legislative remedies and co-operative efforts with our Allies will get underway immediately—aimed at attracting foreign investment and travel to this country—promoting American exports, at stable prices and with more liberal government guarantees and financing—curbing tax and customs loopholes that encourage undue spending of private dollars abroad and sharing with our Allies all efforts to provide for the common defence of the free world and the hopes for growth of the less developed lands. While the current deficit lasts, ways will be found to ease our dollar outlays abroad without placing the full burden on the families of men whom we have asked to serve our flag overseas.

However, we will do what must be done. For our national household is cluttered with unfinished and neglected tasks. Our cities are being engulfed in squalor. Twelve long years after Congress declared our goal to be "a decent home and a suitable environment for every American family," we still have 25 million Americans living in substandard homes. A new housing programme under a new housing and urban affairs department will be needed this year.

Our classrooms contain two million more children than they can properly have room for, taught by 90,000 teachers not properly qualified to teach. One-third of our most promising high school graduates are financially unable to continue the development of their talents. The war babies of the 1940's, who overcrowded our schools in the 1950's, are now descending in the 1960's upon our colleges, with two college students for every one ten years from now, and our colleges are ill-prepared. We lack the scientists, the engineers and the teachers our world obligations require.

Medical research has achieved new wonders—but these wonders are too often beyond the reach of too many people, owing to a lack of income (particularly among the aged), a lack of hospital beds, a lack of nursing homes and a lack of doctors and dentists. Measures to provide health care for the aged under social security, and to increase the supply of both facilities and personnel, must be undertaken this year.

There are other sore spots on the American scene. Our supply of clean water is dwindling. Organised and juvenile crimes cost the taxpayers millions of dollars each year, making it essential that we have improved enforcement and new legislative safeguards. The denial of constitutional rights to some of our fellow Americans on account of race—at the ballot box and elsewhere—disturbs the national conscience, and subjects us to the charge of world opinion that our democracy is not equal to the high promise of our heritage.

But all these problems pale when placed beside those which confront us around the world. No man entering upon this office, regardless of his party, regardless of his previous service in Washington, could fail to be staggered upon learning—even in this brief ten-day period—the harsh enormity of the trials through which we must pass in the next four years. Each day the crises multiply. Each day their solution grows more difficult. Each day we draw nearer the hour of maximum danger, as weapons spread and hostile forces grow stronger. I feel I must inform the Congress that our analyses over the last ten days make it clear that—in each of the principal areas of crisis—the tide of events has been running out and time has not been our friend.

In Asia, the relentless pressures of the Chinese Communists menace the security of the entire area—from the borders of India and South Vietnam to the jungles of Laos, struggling to protect its newly-won independence. We seek in Laos what we seek in all Asia, and, indeed, in all the world—freedom for the people and independence for their government. And this nation shall persevere in our pursuit of these objectives.

In Africa, the Congo has been brutally torn by civil strife, political unrest and public disorder. We shall continue to support the heroic efforts of the United Nations to restore peace and order—efforts which are now endangered by mounting tensions, unsolved problems, and decreasing support from many member states.

In Latin America, Communist agents seeking to exploit that region's peaceful revolution of hope have established a base on Cuba, only 90 miles from our shores. Our objection with Cuba is not over the people's drive for a better life. Our objection is to their domination by foreign and domestic tyrannies. Cuban social and economic reform should be encouraged. Questions of economics and trade policy can always be negotiated. But Communist domination in this hemisphere can never be negotiated.

In Europe our alliances are unfulfilled and in some disarray. The unity of NATO has been weakened by economic rivalry and partially eroded by national interest. It has not yet fully mobilised its resources nor fully achieved a common outlook. Yet no Atlantic power can meet on its own the mutual problems now facing us in defence, foreign aid, monetary reserves, and a host of other areas; and our close ties with those whose hopes and interests we share are among this nation's most powerful assets.

Our greatest challenge is still the world that lies beyond the cold war—but the first great obstacle is still our relations with the Soviet Union and Communist China. We must never be lulled into believing that either Power has yielded its ambitions for world domination—ambitions which they forcefully re-stated only a short time ago. On the contrary, our task is to convince them that aggression and subversion will not be profitable routes to pursue these ends. Open and peaceful competition—for prestige, for markets, for scientific achievements, even for men's minds—is something else again. For if freedom and Communism were to compete for man's allegiance in a world at peace, I would look to the future with ever increasing confidence.

To meet this array of challenges—to fulfil the role we cannot avoid on the world scene—we must re-examine and re-vise our whole arsenal of tools. One must not overshadow the other. On the Presidential coat of arms, the American eagle holds in his right talon the olive branch, while in his left is held a bundle of arrows. We intend to give equal attention to both.

First, we must strengthen our military tools. We are moving into a period of uncertain risk and great commitments in which both the military and diplomatic possibilities require a free world force so powerful as to make any aggression clearly futile. Yet in the past, lack of a consistent, co-herent military strategy, the absence of basic assumptions about our national requirements and the faulty estimate and duplication arising from inter-service rivalries have all made it difficult to assess accurately how adequate—or in-adequate—our defences really are.

I have, therefore, instructed the Secretary of Defence to reappraise our entire defence strategy—our ability to fulfil our commitments—the effectiveness, vulnerability, and dis-persal of our strategic bases, forces and warning systems—the efficiency and economy of our operation and organisa-tion—the elimination of obsolete bases and installations—

and the adequacy, modernisation and mobility of our pres-ent conventional and nuclear forces and weapons systems in the light of present and future dangers.

In the meantime, I have asked the Defence Secretary to initiate immediately three new steps most clearly needed now:

(a) I have directed prompt action to increase our air-lift capacity. Obtaining additional air transport mobility—and obtaining it now—will better assure the ability of our con-ventional forces to respond, with discrimination and speed, to any problem at any spot on the globe at any moment's notice. In particular it will enable us to meet any deliberate effort to avoid or divert our forces by starting limited wars in widely scattered parts of the globe.

(b) I have directed prompt action to step up our Polaris submarine programme. Using unobligated shipbuilding funds now (to let contracts originally scheduled for the next fiscal year) will build and place on station—at least nine months earlier than planned—substantially more units of a crucial deterrent—a fleet that will never attack first, but pos-sess sufficient powers of retaliation, concealed beneath the seas, to discourage any aggressor from launching an attack upon our security.

(c) I have directed prompt action to accelerate our entire missile programme. Until the Secretary of Defence's reap-praisal is completed, the emphasis here will be largely on im-proved organisation and decision-making—on cutting down the wasteful duplications and the time-lag that have handicapped the whole family of missiles. If we are to keep the peace, we need an invulnerable missile force powerful enough to deter any aggressor from even threatening an attack that he would know could not destroy enough of our force to prevent his own destruction. For as I said upon tak-ing the oath of office: "Only when our arms are sufficient beyond doubt can we be certain beyond doubt that they will never be employed."

Secondly, we must improve our economic tools. Our role is essential and unavoidable in the construction of a sound and expanding economy for the entire non-Communist world, helping other nations build the strength to meet their own problems, to satisfy their own aspirations, and to sur-mount their own dangers.

(a) I intend to ask the Congress for authority to establish a new and more effective programme for assisting the eco-nomic, educational and social development of other coun-tries and continents. That programme must stimulate and take more effectively into account the contributions of our Allies, and provide central policy direction for all our own programmes that now so often overlap, conflict or diffuse our energies and resources. Such a programme, compared to past programmes, will require. . . .

More flexibility for short-run emergencies.

More commitment to long-term development.

New attention to education at all levels.

Greater emphasis on the recipient nations' role, their effort, their purpose, with greater social justice for their people, a broader distribution and participation by their people, and more efficient public administration and more efficient tax systems of their own.

And orderly planning for national and regional development instead of a piecemeal approach.

(b) I hope the Senate will take early action approving the convention establishing the Organisation for Economic Co-operation and Development. This will be an important instrument in sharing with our Allies this development effort —working toward the time when each nation will contribute in proportion to its ability to pay. For, while we are prepared to assume our full share of these huge burdens, we cannot and must not be expected to bear them alone.

(c) To our sister republics to the south, we have pledged a new alliance for progress—*alianza para progreso*. Our goal is a free and prosperous Latin America, realising for all its States and all its citizens a degree of economic and social progress that matches their historic contributions of culture, intellect and liberty.

(d) This Administration is expanding its Food-for-Peace programme in every possible way. The product of our abundance must be more effectively used to relieve hunger and help economic growth in all corners of the globe.

(e) An even more valuable national asset is our reservoir of dedicated men and women—not only on our college campuses but in every age group—who have indicated their desire to contribute their skills, their efforts, and a part of their lives to the fight for world order. We can mobilise this talent through the formation of a national peace corps, enlisting the services of all those with desire and capacity to help foreign lands meet their urgent needs for trained personnel.

(f) Finally, while our attention is centred on the development of the non-Communist world, we must never forget our hopes for the ultimate freedom and welfare of the Eastern European peoples. In order to be prepared to help re-establish historic ties of friendship, I am asking the Con-

gress for increased discretion to use economic tools in this area whenever this is found to be clearly in the national interest.

Third, we must sharpen our political and diplomatic tools —the means of co-operation and agreement on which an enforceable world order must ultimately rest.

(a) I have already taken steps to co-ordinate and expand our disarmament effort—to increase our programmes of research and study—and to make arms control a central goal of our national policy under my direction. The deadly arms race, and the huge resources it absorbs, have too long overshadowed all else we must do. We must prevent that arms race from spreading to new nations, to new nuclear powers and to the outer reaches of space. We must make certain that our negotiators are better informed—and better prepared—to formulate workable proposals of our own and to make sound judgments about the proposals of others.

I have asked the other governments concerned to agree to a reasonable delay in the talks on a nuclear test ban—and it is our intention to resume negotiations prepared to reach a final agreement with any nation that is equally willing to agree to an effective and enforceable treaty.

(b) We must increase our support of the United Nations as an instrument to end the cold war instead of an arena in which to fight it. In recognition of its increasing importance and the doubling of its membership:

We are enlarging and strengthening our own missions to the U.N.

We shall help ensure that it is properly financed.

We shall work to see that the integrity of the office of the Secretary-General is maintained.

And I would address a special plea to the smaller nations of the world—to join with us in strengthening this organisation, which is far more essential to their security than it is to ours—the only body in the world today where no nation need be powerful to be secure, where every nation has an equal voice, and where any nation can exert influence not according to the strength of its armies but according to the strength of its ideas. It deserves the support of all.

(c) Finally, this Administration intends to explore promptly all possible areas of co-operation with the Soviet Union and other nations "to invoke the wonders of science instead of its terrors." Specifically, I now invite all nations— including the Soviet Union—to join with us in developing a weather prediction programme, in a new communications satellite programme and in preparation for probing the distant planets of Mars and Venus, probes which may some-day unlock the deepest secrets of the universe.

Today this country is ahead in the science and technology of space, while the Soviet Union is ahead in the capacity to lift large vehicles into orbit. Both nations would help themselves as well as other nations by removing these endeavours from the dark and wasteful competition of the cold war. The United States would be willing to join with the Soviet Union and the scientists of all nations in a greater effort to make the fruits of this new knowledge available to all—and, beyond that, in an effort to extend farm technology to hungry nations—to wipe out disease—to increase the exchanges of scientists and knowledge—and to make our own laboratories available to technicians of other lands who lack the facilities to pursue their own work. Where nature makes natural allies of us all, we can demonstrate that beneficial relations are possible even with those with whom we most deeply disagree—and this must someday be the basis of world peace and world law.

I would like to conclude with a few remarks about the state of the Executive Branch. We have found it full of honest and useful public servants—but their capacity to act decisively at the exact time action is needed has too often been muffled in the morass of committees, timidities and fictitious theories, which have created a growing gap between decision and execution, between planning and reality. In a time of rapidly deteriorating situations at home and abroad, this is bad for the public service and particularly bad for the country; we mean to make a change.

I pledge myself and my colleagues in the Cabinet to a continuous encouragement of initiative, responsibility and energy in serving the public interest. Let every public servant know, whether his post is high or low, that a man's rank and reputation in this Administration will be determined by the size of the job he does, and not by the size of his staff, his office or his budget. Let it be clear that this Administration recognises the value of dissent and daring—that we greet healthy controversy as the hallmark of healthy change. Let the public service be a proud and lively career.

For only through complete dedication by us all to the national interest can we bring our country through the troubled years that lie ahead. Our problems are critical. The tide is unfavourable. The news will be worse before it is better. And while hoping and working for the best, we should prepare ourselves for the worst.

We cannot escape our dangers—neither must we let them drive us into panic or narrow isolation. In many areas of the world where the balance of power already rests with our adversary, the forces of freedom are sharply divided. It is one of the ironies of our time that the techniques of a harsh and repressive system should be able to instill discipline and ardour in its servants—while the blessings of liberty have too often stood for privilege, materialism and a life of ease.

But I have a different view of liberty.

Life in 1961 will not be easy. Wishing it, predicting it, even asking for it, will not make it so. There will be further set-backs before the tide is turned. But turn it we must. The hopes of all mankind rest upon us—not simply upon those of us in this chamber, but upon the peasant in Laos, the fisherman in Nigeria, the exile from Cuba, the spirit that moves every man and nation who shares our hopes for freedom and the future. And in the final analysis, they rest most of all upon the pride and perseverance of our fellow citizens of the great Republic.

New Frontier

Always aware of the power of the press, Kennedy, from his first moments as President, opened much of the White House to photographers, so often considered a nuisance by other Presidents. Now, with entrée to many government offices, the close-up lens of the photographer sent an image of the new atmosphere in the White House to every corner of the globe.

Kennedy's reference to America's standing at a "New Frontier" and his appeal for a fresh start, met with an immediate response both at home and abroad: at the same time it created feelings of anxiety both in America and throughout the world. The new foreign policy of the United States was to be based on the principle of increased military strength, coupled with the will to negotiate at all times. The formula "We are ready to defend our interests but we are also ready to negotiate" gave rise to much uncertainty and doubt, particularly in the German Federal Republic, and this was to overshadow the President's entire term of office. The armaments programme announced on July 26th, 1961, should have resolved such doubts, since it sought to make good the deficiencies of the eight years of the Eisenhower Administration, and it did in fact achieve this. The space exploration programme was also agreed upon and speeded up, with its first great success on October 4th, 1962, when Commander Schirra orbited the earth six times.

The crux of the New Frontier programme was a plan to develop the American economy in keeping with its inherent capacities. The income tax system was to be reformed in order to stimulate private investment, mobilise a fund of good will and expand foreign trade on the European model. By virtue of the Trade Expansion Act passed by Congress in September 1962, Kennedy hoped to bring about an Atlantic trade interchange. This was to be done by the United Kingdom's joining the European Economic Community, so creating a vast European market to compete with the American, and by a general lowering of tariffs. This was intended to strengthen the Atlantic community and to guarantee lasting prosperity in the West, while massive schemes of aid for underdeveloped nations were to result in a gradual improvement of living standards everywhere. The first round of this plan was wrecked by the French veto of the U.K. entry into the Common Market, and by the protectionist tendencies of the Economic Authority in Brussels.

Kennedy aimed to give new form and content to Foreign Aid and Aid for Develop-

It is 7.45 p.m. The President leaves his office, a bundle of newspapers under his arm for his evening reading.

Left: The President presides over a meeting of his Scientific Advisory Committee, which is made up of brilliant scientists from many different fields. The President seeks their advice on various problems. The decisions are his alone.

Secretary of Defence, Robert McNamara, Vice-President Lyndon B. Johnson and President Kennedy discuss national defence problems. Because of his back injuries the President prefers to sit in a rocking chair.

President Kennedy discusses foreign policy with his Secretary of State, Dean Rusk.

ment. As one instrument of this policy he formed the Peace Corps, which he entrusted to his brother-in-law, Sargent Shriver, and which relied entirely on young America's spirit of idealism.

There were further plans for making effective use of all the available resources of the nation—the improvement of the whole system of primary schools and of higher education by Federal action, the extension of medical facilities for the aged and needy, and the elimination of unemployment in distressed areas.

Despite the fact that it emerged with strong Democratic majorities in the 1960 and 1962 elections, Congress followed the President's lead either reluctantly or not at all. For the isolationists and conservative business circles Kennedy remained ever an enemy. Hostility mounted to unprecedented heights when in 1962 he vetoed the steel industry's decision to fix arbitrary price increases, and also in July 1963, when he proposed a special tax on overseas investments to reverse the balance of payments deficit.

About halfway through his term of office the problem of human and civic rights began increasingly to cast a shadow over Kennedy's efforts on the domestic front. In September 1962, he hammered home the supremacy of the law against the Governor of Mississippi, when he tried to prevent a negro enrolling in the State University. In the summer of 1963, Kennedy laid before Congress the Civil Rights Bill, thereby taking what he hoped would be a decisive step towards legal, moral and practical equality for all American citizens. He did not live to see the results. Kennedy conducted an untiring campaign against traditional injustices, outmoded customs and ingrained prejudices. This was the secret of his appeal to liberal American youth. In a fundamentally conservative country his thoughts and actions seemed revolutionary, all the more since some of his colleagues, through the manner and timing of their proposals, seemed resolved to jerk people out of their apathy even if it meant giving offense. Kennedy, for his own part, was content to take a more moderate and patient attitude. As one of the shrewdest and most alert politicians ever produced by the United States, he was fully aware of the most sensitive spots of the electorate: but once he was persuaded of the need of a certain course of action in the national interest, the mere risk of unpopularity could not deter him.

Light shines into the dark garden of the White House from the brightly lit office of the President. Late in the night Kennedy confers with Walt Whitman Rostow, the Deputy Special Assistant for National Security.

A meeting of the Atomic Energy Commission at the White House has ended. The President leaves the room while the scientists finish their talks.

44

The sticking plaster over Kennedy's left eyebrow hides a small wound the President received banging his head against a table top while lifting up a toy for his daughter Caroline.

One of the best known figures of the new Administration, Pierre Salinger, Kennedy's Press Secretary, is a trusted confidant of the President.

Defence

On the occasion of his visit to Germany in summer of 1963, the President inspected units of American troops stationed in Western Germany. In October of 1961, at Fort Bragg, President Kennedy personally reviewed the degree of training of the Airborne troops and drove past the ranks of the 82nd Airborne Division (below).

We dare not tempt them with weakness.
For only when our arms are sufficient beyond doubt
can we be certain beyond doubt that they will
never be employed.

A special X-15 rocket research plane flies over the salt runway of Edwards Air Force base in California prior to landing. The promotion of the rocket programme was among the most urgent concerns of the Kennedy Administration.

On October 22nd, 1963, troops were flown non-stop from an air base in Texas to Germany. This manoeuvre, Operation Big Lift, was to prove to the Europeans that the U.S.A. was on the alert at all danger points in spite of relaxed world tension.

Right: At many American army depots there are sufficient materials and weapons to build up a striking force at short notice. During the "Big Lift" these tanks near Kaiserslautern were taken over by troops of the 2nd Division, immediately after landing, and moved to forward areas.

Space Programme

Preceding pages:

Left: President Kennedy accelerated the construction of nuclear powered submarines which make up the core of America's defensive force. Able to cruise under water for months, these nuclear armed submarines can retaliate against surprise attack on the U.S. or its allies.

Centre: Bombers of the Strategic Air Command (S.A.C.) stay constantly airborne to be prepared against any sudden attack.

Right: A Matador guided missile on its test flight. Guided by electronic brains, these missiles are capable of carrying nuclear warheads hundreds of miles to their targets.

Left, above: The space capsule Friendship 7 with the astronaut John H. Glenn on board comes down in the Atlantic Ocean after circling the earth three times.

Right, above: On February 20th, 1962, Friendship 7 is taken on board the destroyer Noa.

Right, below: The automatic cinema camera recorded astronaut Glenn eating apple puree from a tube during the flight.

Astronaut John H. Glenn, who orbited the earth three times in February 1962, explains the mechanism of the space capsule Friendship 7 to President Kennedy and Vice-President Johnson.

The mirrors on the chest and forearms of the astronaut reflect the dials of the instruments on to the lens of the cinema camera which is directed on the astronaut during the whole flight.

Let both sides seek to invoke the wonders of science instead of its terrors. Together let us explore the stars, conquer the deserts, eradicate disease, tap the ocean depths and encourage the arts and commerce.

A historic picture. The Atlas rocket carrying space capsule Friendship 7 with the astronaut John H. Glenn into orbit leaves its base at Cape Canaveral.

At a tour of inspection of the Research Laboratories of the Atomic Energy Commission in Nevada, the President was shown the "Beetle". This machine, which is automatic and remote controlled, is used for the transport of radioactive material.

FROM PRESIDENT KENNEDY'S
ADDRESS TO CLERGY, HOUSTON, TEXAS

September 12th, 1960

So it is apparently necessary for me to state once again—not what kind of church I believe in, for that should be important only to me—but what kind of America I believe in.

I believe in an America where the separation of Church and State is absolute—where no Catholic prelate would tell the President (should he be Catholic) how to act, and no Protestant minister would tell his parishioners for whom to vote—where no church or church school is granted any public funds or political preference—and where no man is denied public office merely because his religion differs from the President who might appoint him or the people who might elect him.

I believe in an America that is officially neither Catholic, Protestant nor Jewish—where no public official either requests or accepts instructions on public policy from the Pope, the National Council of Churches or any other ecclesiastical source—where no religious body seeks to impose its will directly or indirectly upon the general populace or the public acts of its officials—and where religious liberty is so indivisible that an act against one church is treated as an act against all.

For while this year it may be a Catholic against whom the finger of suspicion is pointed, in other years it has been, and may someday be again, a Jew—or a Quaker—or a Unitarian—or a Baptist. Today I may be the victim—but tomorrow it may be you.

Finally, I believe in an America where religious intolerance will someday end—where all men and all churches are treated as equal—where every man has the same right to attend or not attend the church of his choice—where there is no Catholic vote, no anti-Catholic vote, no bloc voting of any kind—and where Catholics, Protestants and Jews, at both the lay and pastoral level, will refrain from those attitudes of disdain and division which have so often marred their works in the Past, and promote instead the American ideal of brotherhood.

That is the kind of America in which I believe. And it represents the kind of Presidency in which I believe—a great office that must neither be humbled by making it the instrument of any one religious group nor tarnished by arbitrarily witholding its occupancy from the members of any one religious group. I believe in a President whose religious views are his own private affair, neither imposed by him upon the Nation nor imposed by the Nation upon him as a condition to holding that office.

I want a Chief Executive whose public acts are responsible to all groups and obligated to none—who can attend any ceremony, service, or dinner his office may appropriately require of him—and whose fulfillment of his Presidential oath is not limited or conditioned by any religious oath, ritual or obligation.

I am wholly opposed to the State being used by any religious group, Catholic or Protestant, to compel, prohibit, or persecute the free exercise of any other religion. And I hope that you and I condemn with equal fervour those nations which deny their Presidency to Protestants and those which deny it to Catholics. And rather than cite the misdeeds of those who differ, I would cite the record of the Catholic Church in such nations as Ireland and France—and the independance of such statesmen as Adenauer and de Gaulle.

But let me stress again that these are my views—for, contrary to common newspaper usage, I am not the Catholic candidate for President. I am the Democratic Party's candidate for President who happens also to be a Catholic. I do not speak for my Church on public matters—and the Church does not speak for me.

Whatever issue may come before me as President—on birth control, divorce, censorship, gambling or any other subject—I will make my decision in accordance with these views, in accordance with what my conscience tells me to be the national interest, and without regard to outside religious pressures or dictates. And no power or threat of punishment could cause me to decide otherwise.

But if the time should ever come—and I do not concede any conflict to be even remotely possible—when my office would require me to either violate my conscience or violate the national interest, then I would resign the office; and I hope any conscientious public servant would do the same.

But I do not intend to apologize for these views to my critics of either Catholic or Protestant faith—nor do I intend to disavow either my views or my Church in order to win this election.

If I should lose on the real issues, I shall return to my seat in the Senate, satisfied that I had tried my best and was fairly judged. But if this election is decided on the basis that 40 million Americans lost their chance of being President on the day they were baptized, then it is the whole Nation that will be the loser, in the eyes of Catholics and non-Catholics around the world, in the eyes of history, and in the eyes of our own people.

FROM PRESIDENT KENNEDY'S SPEECH TO THE AMERICAN PEOPLE

July 25th, 1961

Seven weeks ago tonight I returned from Europe to report on my meeting with Premier Khrushchev and the others. His grim warning about the future of the world, his aide memoire on Berlin, the subsequent speeches and threats which he and his agents have launched, and the increase in the Soviet military budget that he has announced have all prompted a series of decisions by this Administration and a series of consultations with the members of NATO.

In Berlin, as you recall, he intends to bring to an end, through the stroke of the pen, first our legal rights to be in West Berlin, and secondly, our ability to make good on our commitment to the two million people of that city. That we cannot permit.

West Berlin, lying exposed 110 miles inside of East Germany, surrounded by Soviet troops and close to Soviet supply lines, has many roles. It is more than a showcase of liberty, a symbol, an island of freedom in a Communist sea. It is even more than a link with the free world, a beacon of hope behind the Iron Curtain, an escape hatch for refugees.

West Berlin is all that. But above all it has now become, as never before, the great testing place of Western courage and will, a focal point where our solemn commitments, stretching back over the years since 1945, and Soviet ambitions now meet in basic confrontation.

It would be a mistake for others to look upon Berlin, because of its location, as a tempting target. The United States is there; the United Kingdom and France are there; the pledge of NATO is there and the people of Berlin are there. It is as secure in that sense as the rest of us, for we cannot separate its safety from our own.

I hear it said that West Berlin is militarily untenable. And so was Bastogne and so, in fact, was Stalingrad. Any dangerous spot is tenable if men, brave men, will make it so.

We do not want to fight, but we have fought before and others in earlier times have made the same dangerous mistake of assuming that the West was too selfish and too soft and too divided to resist invasions of freedom in other lands.

Those who threaten to unleash the forces of war on a dispute over West Berlin should recall the words of the ancient philosopher: "A man who causes fear cannot be free from fear."

We cannot and will not permit the Communists to drive us out of Berlin, either gradually or by force. For the fulfilment of our pledge to that city is essential to the morale and security of West Germany, to the unity of Western Europe, and to the faith of the entire free world. Soviet strategy has long been aimed, not merely at Berlin, but at dividing and neutralising all of Europe, forcing us back to our own shores. We must meet our oft-stated pledge to the free people of West Berlin, and maintain our rights and their safety, even in the face of force, in order to maintain the confidence of other free peoples in our word and our resolve. The strength of the Alliance on which our security depends is dependent in turn on our willingness to meet our commitments to them.

So long as the Communists insist that they are preparing to end by themselves, unilaterally, our rights in West Berlin and our commitments to its people, we must be prepared to defend those rights and those commitments. We will at all times be ready to talk, if talk will help. But we must also be ready to resist with force, if force is used upon us. Either alone will fail. Together, they can serve the cause of freedom and peace.

The new preparations that we shall make to defend the peace are part of the long-term build-up in our strength. They are based on our needs to meet a world-wide threat, on a basis which stretches far beyond the present Berlin crisis.

A first need is to hasten progress toward the military goals which the North Atlantic Allies have set for themselves. In Europe today nothing less will suffice. We will put even greater resources into fulfilling those goals and we look to our Allies to do the same.

The supplementary defence build-ups that I asked from the Congress in March and May have already started moving us toward these and other defence goals. They included an increase in the size of the Marine Corps, improved readiness of our reserves, expansion of our air and sea lift, and stepped-up procurement of needed weapons, ammunition, and other items. To ensure a continuing invulnerable capacity to deter or destroy any aggressor, they provided for the strengthening of our missile power and for putting 50 per cent of our B-52 and B-47 bombers on a ground alert which would send them on their way with 15 minutes warning.

These measures must be speeded up, and still others must now be taken. We must have sea and airlift capable of moving our forces quickly and in large numbers to any part of the world.

But even more importantly, we need the capability of placing in any critical area at the appropriate time a force which, combined with those of our Allies, is large enough to make clear our determination and our ability to defend our rights at all costs—and to meet all levels of aggressor pressure with whatever levels of force are required. We intend to have a wider choice than humiliation or all-out nuclear action.

As signers of the UN Charter, we shall always be prepared to discuss international problems with any and all nations that are willing to talk, and listen, with reason. If they have proposals—not demands—we shall hear them. If they seek genuine understanding—not concessions of our rights—we shall meet with them.

We have previously indicated our readiness to remove any actual irritants in West Berlin, but the freedom of that city is not negotiable. We cannot negotiate with those who say, "What's mine is mine and what's yours is negotiable." But we are willing to consider any arrangement or treaty in Germany consistent with the maintenance of peace and freedom, and with the legitimate security interest of all nations.

We recognise the Soviet Union's historical concerns about their security in Central and Eastern Europe, after a series of ravaging invasions—and we believe arrangements can be worked out which will help to meet those concerns, and make it possible for both security and freedom to exist in this troubled area.

For it is not the freedom of West Berlin which is "abnormal" in Germany today, but the situation in that entire divided country. If anyone doubts the legality of our rights in Berlin, we are ready to have it submitted to international adjudication. If anyone doubts the extent to which our presence is desired by the people of West Berlin, compared to East German feelings about their regime, we are ready to have that question submitted to a free vote in Berlin and, if possible, among all the German people. And let us hear at that time from the 2½ million refugees who have fled the Communist regime in East Germany, voting for Western-type freedom with their feet.

The world is not deceived by the Communist attempt to label Berlin as a hot-bed of war. There is peace in Berlin today. The source of world trouble and tension is Moscow, not Berlin. And if war begins, it will have begun in Moscow, and not Berlin.

For the choice of peace or war is largely theirs, not ours. It is the Soviets who have stirred up this crisis. It is they who are trying to force a change. It is they who have opposed free elections. It is they who have rejected an all-German peace treaty and the rulings of international law. And as Americans know from our history on our own old frontier, gun battles are caused by outlaws, and not by officers of the peace.

In short, while we are ready to defend our interests, we shall also be ready to search for peace, in quiet exploratory talks, in formal or informal meetings. We do not want military considerations to dominate the thinking of either East or West. And Mr. Khrushchev may find that his invitation to other nations to join in a meaningless treaty may lead to their inviting him to join in the community of peaceful men, in abandoning the use of force, and in respecting the sanctity of agreements.

We in the West must move together in building military strength. We must consult one another more closely than ever before. We must together design our proposals for peace, and labour together as they are pressed at the conference table. And together we must share the burdens and the risks of this effort.

The Atlantic Community, as we know it, has been built in response to challenges: the challenges of European chaos of 1947; of the Berlin blockade in 1948; and the challenge of Communist aggression in Korea in 1950. Now, standing strong and prosperous, after an unprecedented decade of progress, the Atlantic Community will not forget either its history or the principles which give it meaning.

The solemn vow each of us gave to West Berlin in time of peace will not be broken in time of danger. If we do not meet our commitments to Berlin, where will we later stand? If we are not true to our word there, all that we have achieved in collective security, which relies on these words, will mean nothing, and if there is one path above all others to war, it is the path of weakness and disunity.

Today the endangered frontier of freedom runs through divided Berlin. We want it to remain a frontier of peace. This is the hope of every citizen of the Atlantic Community, every citizen of Eastern Europe, and, I am confident, every citizen of the Soviet Union, for I cannot believe that the Russian people—who bravely suffered enormous losses in the Second World War—would now wish to see the peace upset once more in Germany. The Soviet Government alone can convert Berlin's frontier of peace into a pretext for war.

The steps I have indicated tonight are aimed at avoiding the war. To sum it all up: we seek peace—but we shall not surrender. That is the central meaning of this crisis—and the meaning of your Government's policy.

With your help, and the help of other free men, this crisis can be surmounted. Freedom can prevail—and peace can endure.

FROM THE TRANSCRIPT OF AN INTERVIEW GIVEN BY PRESIDENT KENNEDY TO MR. ALEKSEI ADZHUBEI, EDITOR OF "IZVESTIA"

November 25th, 1961

I think that the Soviet Union and the United States should live together in peace.

Where we feel the difficulty comes is the effort by the Soviet Union to communise, in a sense, the entire world. If the Soviet Union were merely seeking to protect its own national interests, to protect its own national security, and would permit other countries to live as they wish—to live in peace—then I believe that the problems which now cause so much tension would fade away.

We want the people of the Soviet Union to live in peace—we want the same for our own people. It is this effort to push outward the Communist system, on to country after country, that represents, I think, the great threat to peace.

People want to live in different ways, that is what we want, also. If they have a fair opportunity to make a choice, if they choose to support Communism, we accept that. What we object to is the attempt to impose Communism by force, or a situation where once a people may have fallen under Communism, the Communists do not give them a fair opportunity to make another choice.

To divide a country, to divide a city, to put up a wall in a city, we believe, only increase tensions rather than diminish them. And we believe that, if the German people were permitted to be unified, adequate steps could be taken to protect the security of all involved.

Now we recognise that today the Soviet Union does not intend to permit reunification, and that as long as the Soviet Union has that policy, Germany will not be reunified. The question now is whether the Soviet Union will sign a treaty with the East German authorities which will increase tension rather than diminish it. As I said in my speech at the United Nations, we recognise that the Soviet Union can sign any treaty it wishes with the East German authorities. What we find to be so dangerous, however, is the claim that that treaty will deny us our rights in West Berlin, rights which we won through the war, rights which were agreed to by the Soviet Union, the United States, Britain and France, and which we believe should be continued.

But if you sign a treaty with East Germany and those rights are subject to the wishes of the East German authorities, it seems to me that that is going to increase tension. If the Soviet Union attempts in that treaty to turn over jurisdiction over West Berlin to the East German authorities, against the wishes of the people of West Berlin—if the lines of communication and access, from West Berlin to the outside world and the West, are completely under the control of East German authorities to cut any time they so wish—then this treaty does not bring peace, it only increases the danger.

Now I am hopeful that, in the conversations and negotiations which we hope to have with the Soviet Union, assurances will be given which will permit us to continue to exercise the rights which we now have in West Berlin, as a result of the existing four-Power agreement, and will permit free access in and out of the city. We do not want to stay in West Berlin if the people there do not want us to stay. But they want us to stay. When they decide that they don't want us, we will leave.

But as long as they wish us to stay, it seems to me that the rights which are ours by agreement should be maintained. I am hopeful that the Soviet Union will agree with this, and in particular will agree to permit supplies and people to move in and out of West Berlin freely. Then we can in my opinion, reach a peaceful settlement in the centre of Europe, and if we can reach an agreement on this question, then I believe our relations will greatly improve.

The reason why we have been reluctant to recognise East Germany as a sovereign power is that we do not recognise the division of Germany. In our opinion the German people wish to have one united country. If the Soviet Union had lost the war, the Soviet people themselves would object to a line being drawn through Moscow and the entire country. If we had been defeated in war, we wouldn't like to have a line drawn down the Mississippi river. The Germans want to be united. I think it should be possible to provide for that under conditions which will protect the interests of all concerned. But the Soviet Union believes that it is more in their interest to keep Germany divided.

All we wish to do is maintain a very limited—and they are a very limited number of troops of the three Powers in West Berlin and to have, for example, an international administration on the autobahn so that goods and people can move freely in and out. Then we can have peace in this area for years.

If I were a Soviet veteran, I would see that West Germany now has only nine divisions, which is a fraction of the Soviet forces. Nine divisions. It has no nuclear weapons of its own. It has a very small air force—almost no navy, I think perhaps two or three submarines. So it is not a military threat. Its nine divisions are under the international control of NATO, and subject to the command of the NATO organisation, which is made up of 15 countries of Europe which altogether have, in West Germany now, about 22 or 23 divisions—about the same number as the Soviet divisions in East Germany. So that I do not see that this country represents a military threat now to the Soviet Union, even though I recognise how bitter was the struggle in World War II—in the same way that Japan today represents no threat to the United States, even though 20 years ago there were four years of war in the Pacific against the Japanese. The power of countries changes—weapons change—science changes—without missiles, without nuclear capability, with very few divisions, today, I don't believe West Germany is a military threat.

Then I would look at the power of the United States, and I would look at the power of the Soviet Union, and I would say that the important thing is for the Soviet Union and the United States not to get into a war, which would destroy both of our systems. So as a Soviet veteran, I would want the Soviet Union to reach an agreement with the United States which recognises the interests and the commitments of the United States, as well as our own, and not attempt to enforce single-handedly a new situation upon the United States which would be against previous commitments we had made. The Soviet Union made a commitment in regard to Berlin in 1945. Germany today is divided. Germany today is not a threat to the Soviet Union militarily.

So, if I were a Soviet officer and wanted peace, I would think peace can be won and my country's security can be assured. The Soviet Union is a strong military power. It has great nuclear capacity. It has missiles, planes—it has a great number of divisions—it has countries associated with it. No one is ever going to invade the Soviet Union again. There is no military power that can do that. The problem is to make an agreement which will permit us to have our interests recognised, as well as yours. That should not be beyond the capacity of us both.

Chairman Khrushchev did not, nor did I, make the arrangements in 1945 in regard to Berlin. Our responsibility is to bring about peace, and I believe it can be done.

The United States, as a matter of national policy, as I said at the United Nations, will not give nuclear weapons to any country, and I would be extremely reluctant to see West Germany acquire a nuclear capacity of its own. Chancellor Adenauer stated that they would not, in 1954. That is still the policy of that government, and I think that is the wise policy.

That is why I believe it to be so important to stress the West German army is integrated in NATO. NATO is now commanded by an American; and, in my judgment, as long as German forces are integrated in NATO, and NATO is under the control of the 15 NATO countries, none of which wants another war—there is security for all. And I think that will continue.

Now if this situation changed, if Germany developed an atomic capability of its own, if it developed many missiles, or a strong national army that threatened war, then I would understand your concern, and I would share it.

The real danger today is the fact that both of us possess in our nuclear stockpiles the means to impose great devastation upon each other—and we are the ones that have the most to lose from war.

FROM THE ACCEPTANCE ADDRESS
DEMOCRATIC NATIONAL CONVENTION

July 15th, 1960

. . . For the problems are not all solved and the battles are not all won—and we stand today on the edge of a new frontier—the frontier of the 1960's—a frontier of unknown opportunities and perils—a frontier of unfulfilled hopes and threats.

Woodrow Wilson's New Freedom promised our nation a new political and economic framework. Franklin Roosevelt's New Deal promised security and succour to those in need. But the New Frontier of which I speak is not a set of promises—it is a set of challenges. It sums up not what I intend to offer the American people, but what I intend to ask of them. It appeals to their pride, not their pocketbook —it holds out the promise of more sacrifice instead of more security.

. . . Can a nation organized and governed such as ours endure? That is the real question. Have we the nerve and the will? Can we carry through in an age where we will witness not only new breakthroughs in weapons of destruction but also a race for mastery of the sky and the rain, the ocean and the tides, the far side of space and the inside of men's minds?

The Economy

Nearly one-eighth of those who are without jobs live almost without hope in nearly one hundred especially depressed and troubled areas. The rest include new school graduates unable to use their talents, farmers forced to give up the part-time jobs that balanced their budgets, skilled and unskilled workers laid off in such important industries as metals, machinery, automobiles and apparel.

"No Work". The piece of cardboard with these clumsily written words is fastened on a door in the mining district of West Virginia. From the very beginning of Kennedy's Presidency his Administration was faced with the problems of unemployment and economic depression in this, the world's richest country.

Executive Order No. 1, decreed by the new President on his first day in office, applied to the unemployed in those parts of the U.S. hit by economic depression. It doubled the delivery of free food parcels to needy unemployed. Here, in Detroit, an official of the Public Welfare Office gives out food rations.

Next to industrial workers, farmers were the principal victims of economic recession in the U.S. Since 1951 the farmers' incomes had decreased by 25%. Many farmers had to give up their property and seek employment in areas where they came up against opposition from workers fearing for their own jobs. The Kennedy Administration tried to master the situation with an extensive programme providing an improvement in unemployment pay, a generous distribution of free food, industrialisation of undeveloped regions, the promotion of the house-building scheme, the raising of minimum wages, and the bettering of farming conditions.

Secretary of State Udall talking with an American-Indian woman and a State official. The Indians on the Reservations are among the most economically backward groups in the U.S.

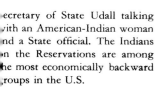

A worker in Detroit getting his weekly unemployment pay.

The Attorney General, Rober[t]
Kennedy, in his office.

A white man, demonstrating i[n]
Alabama for the rights of th[e]
negroes, is carried off by police[-]
men.

Civil Rights

We preach freedom over the world, and we mean it, and we cherish our freedom here at home, but are we to say to the world and, much more importantly, to each other that this is a land of the free except for the Negroes; that we have no second class citizens except Negroes; that we have no class or caste system, no ghettoes, no master race except with respect to Negroes?

The Kennedy Administration saw the greatest campaign for equal rights by the American negroes in the nation's history, and rose to its support. In 1961 severe rioting broke out when coloured and white demonstrators drove through various southern States in the same bus, protesting against the colour barriers in public transportation. One tour of these "Freedom Riders" ended cruelly when in Montgomery, Alabama, they were attacked and beaten up by segregationists (right). More violence flared up in spring of 1963, especially in Birmingham, Alabama, where coloured residents demonstrated against segregated restaurants and shops. Police Chief Eugene "Bull" Connor used police dogs and fire hoses to disperse demonstrators. This in turn brought larger demonstrations in other Southern States. In Birmingham, a moderate Mayor Boutwell gradually restored racial peace. Not so in Alabama where Governor George C. Wallace tried to prevent two coloured students from entering the Alabama State University, despite a Federal Court order integrating the school. President Kennedy subdued this resistance by nationalising Alabama State forces, thus compelling Wallace to back down.

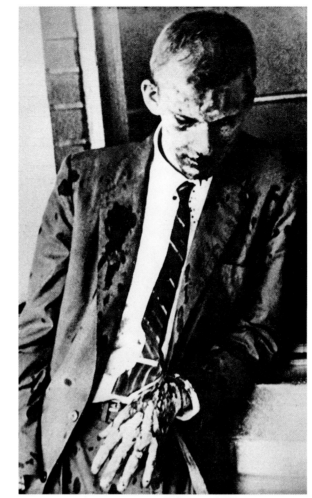

Below: Some observers called it a peaceful revolution. On August 28th, 1963, about 200,000 coloured and white citizens staged a quiet and dignified march in the nation's capital to stress their claim for equal civil rights.

Right: In contrast to the majority of peaceful demonstrations, tension reached its climax after the assassination of negro leader Medgar Evers at Jackson, Mississippi, on June 12th, 1963. Jeering at the local police after Evers' murder by a white fanatic, these negroes are demanding protection from violence. Fortunately, a May 24th secret meeting called by Attorney General Robert Kennedy and attended by negro leaders, had already started to chart the way towards the end of racial strife. This, together with the firm attitude of the United States Supreme Court and the resolute intervention of President Kennedy, brought a marked easing of racial tension during the following months.

Above: Dr. Martin Luther King, leader of the passive resistance movement for the assertion of negro rights making a speech.

Left: The mass-meeting on August 28th, 1963, in front of Lincoln Memorial, was organised mainly with a view to drawing the attention of Congress to the urgency of the Civil Rights Bill, which had been brought before Congress by President Kennedy on June 19th.

Right: No President since Abraham Lincoln had done as much as President Kennedy to foster the rights of the negro. Even at the risk of losing important southern votes he interceded against Governor Wallace in summer 1963, urged Congress to pass his Civil Rights Bill, and demanded that American industrial leaders treat coloured and white citizens alike. In this struggle his chief lieutenant was his brother Robert Kennedy.

Peace Corps

To those people in the huts and villages of half the globe struggling to break the bonds of mass misery, we pledge our best efforts to help them help themselves, for whatever period is required—not because the Communists may be doing it, not because we seek their votes, but because it is right. If a free society cannot help the many who are poor, it cannot save the few who are rich.

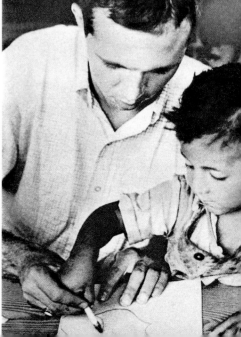

The Peace Corps was one of the new President's outstanding programmes. Calling first on young, and later on older American citizens to donate their services and skills to help less fortunate nations, the Corps received 17,300 applications in its first three weeks of existence. Headed by Sargent Shriver, a Kennedy brother-in-law, Peace Corps units are at work throughout the world. Shown here is Shriver talking to a Nigerian delegation and other Corps officials. The facing pictures show young Americans working with the Peace Corps in Peru.

*The energy, the faith, the devotion
which we bring to this endeavour will
light our country and all who serve it
—and the glow from that fire can
truly light the world.*

A United States Information Service official surrounded by children in the tiny village of Bam Done, in Laos.

FROM THE TRANSCRIPT OF A TELEVISION INTERVIEW

December 18th, 1962

Following is the text of the transcript of a national television programme in which President Kennedy was interviewed last night at the White House by Mr. William Lawrence, of the American Broadcasting Company; Mr. George Herman of the Columbia Broadcasting System; and Mr. Sander Vanocur of the National Broadcasting Company.

Q.: As you look back upon your first two years in office, Sir, has your experience in the office matched your expectations?

President Kennedy: Well, I think in the first place the problems are more difficult than I had imagined they were. Secondly, there is a limitation upon the ability of the United States to solve these problems. We are involved now in the Congo in a very difficult situation. We have been unable to secure an implementation of the policy which we have supported. We are involved in a good many other areas. We are trying to see if a solution can be found to the struggle between Pakistan and India, with whom we want to maintain friendly relations. Yet they are unable to come to an agreement. There is a limitation, in other words, upon the power of the United States to bring about solutions.

I think our people get awfully impatient and may be fatigued and tired, and saying "We have been carrying this burden for seventeen years; can we lay it down?" We can't lay it down, and I don't see how we are going to lay it down in this century.

So that I would say that the problems are more difficult than I had imagined them to be. The responsibilities placed on the United States are greater than I imagined them to be, and there are greater limitations upon our ability to bring about a favourable result than I had imagined them to be. And I think that is probably true of anyone who becomes President, because there is such a difference between those who advise or speak or legislate and between the man who must select from the various alternatives proposed and say that this shall be the policy of the United States. It is much easier to make the speeches than it is to finally make the judgments, because unfortunately your advisers are frequently divided. If you take the wrong course, and on occasion I have, the President bears the burden of the responsibility quite rightly.

Q.: Mr. President, have you noted since you have been in office that this terrible responsibility for the fate of mankind has, notwithstanding the differences that divide you, drawn you and Mr. Khrushchev somewhat closer in this joint sense of responsibility? He seems to betray it, especially in his speech to the Supreme Soviet earlier.

A.: I think in that speech this week he showed his awareness of the nuclear age, but of course, the Cuban effort has made it more difficult for us to carry out any successful negotiations, because this was an effort to materially change the balance of power. It was done in secret, steps were taken really to deceive us by every means they could, and they were planning in November to open to the world the fact that they had these missiles so close to the United States; not that they were intending to fire them, because if they were going to get into a nuclear struggle, they have their own missiles in the Soviet Union. But it would have politically changed the balance of power. It would have appeared to, and appearances contribute to reality. So it is going to be some time before it is possible for us to come to any real understanding with Mr. Khrushchev. But I do think his speech shows that he realises how dangerous a world we live in.

The real problem is the Soviet desire to expand their power and influence. If Mr. Khrushchev would concern himself with the real interests of the people of the Soviet Union, that they have a higher standard of living, to protect his own security, there is no real reason why the United States and the Soviet Union, separated by so many thousands of miles and land and water, both rich countries, both with very energetic people, should not be able to live in peace. But it is this constant determination which the Chinese show in the most militant form, and which the Soviets also have shown that they will not settle for that kind of a peaceful world, but must settle for a Communist world. That is what makes the real danger; the combination of these two systems in conflict around the world in a nuclear age is what makes the sixties so dangerous.

Q.: Mr. President, a lot of people have said that it is necessary, and these are a lot of the demonologists who have some knowledge about the Soviet Union, that it is necessary for an American President to protect Mr. Khrushchev, because he is the best Soviet Prime Minister we will ever get. Do you feel that is really the duty of an American President or it is the duty of an American President to protect the national interest?

A.: No, I don't think it is our duty to protect Mr. Khrushchev. This argument that his successor would be worse: I don't know what his successor will be like. What I think is our duty is to try to protect our vital interests, protect the security of the free world, and have Mr. Khrushchev understand our intentions clearly enough so that he can proceed about his business in a way which does not threaten our security, and does not bring a war. We don't want to have to protect our security by means of war. But Mr. Khrushchev has to understand that there are vital interests in the United States for which we will fight, and if he will come, he and the Communists and the Soviet Union, will come to devote their energies to demonstrating how their system works in the Soviet Union, it seems to me his vital interests are easily protected with the power that he has, and we could have a long period of peace. Then we could make a judgment which system does the job. We believe ours does. He has argued that his does, internally. But instead, by these constant desires to change the balance of power in the world, that is what, it seems to me, introduces the dangerous element.

Now, I do think in fairness, if you read his speech this week, you can see that we would be far worse off—the world would be—if the Chinese dominated the Communist movement, because they believe in war as the means of bringing about the Communist world. Mr. Khrushchev's means are destruction, but he believes that peaceful co-existence and support of these wars of liberation, small wars, will bring about our defeat. The Chinese Communists believe that by constantly hitting, and if war comes, a nuclear Third World War, they can survive it anyway with 750 million people. So we are better off with the Khrushchev view than we are with the Chinese Communist view, quite obviously. But Mr. Khrushchev does not wish us well, unfortunately.

Q.: Is there anything we can do to influence this growing split within the Communist bloc, or should we just tend to the world that we have, and make sure that it is not ripe for Communist penetration?

A.: I think that this dispute which has become intensified is a matter that I think if we would, as you suggest, devote our attention to so much of the world which is in very desperate condition. Some of the countries of Latin America, Africa, Asia, which need our assistance, which need our support, if we do our job of strengthening the free world, then we will be, it seems to me, creating pressure, a counter-pressure against the Communist advance, and that Communism internally, under that kind of pressure, will find its lot more difficult.

I do think we have a tendency to think of the world as Communist and free, as if it were two units. The fact of the matter is our world is so divided, so poverty-stricken, so desperate in many conditions, that we have a full-time job just strengthening the section of the world which is not Communist, all of Africa, newly independent and poverty-stricken. Here we have the Prime Minister of Somali who came the other day, $45 per year the per capita income. The average wage in United States manufacture is about $94 a week. $45 a year. Well, now, he has got staggering problems. Through Latin America and parts of North-East Brazil, $100 a year they are living on. So we have got a big job to do in our own area. If we can strengthen that area—as Communism in my opinion is completely fallacious and really is a system which really does not suit the desires of the average man—then I think we can be successful.

Q.: How do you as the leader of the Western Alliance, of the strongest member nation, how do you get the European countries, which are becoming increasingly more independent, increasingly more prosperous, which is what you said you hoped they could become, how do you get them to follow your lead?

A.: In the first place you can do your part. We are doing our part. We have our troops in Western Europe, they are the best equipped; we have six divisions, which is about a fourth of all of the divisions on the Western front. They are the best equipped. They can fight tomorrow, which is not true of most of the other units. So we are doing our part there, and we are also providing the largest naval force in the world. We are also providing the nuclear force in the world, and we are also carrying out the major space programme for the free world, as well as carrying the whole burden in South Vietnam. We hope Western Europe will make a greater effort on its own, both in developing conventional forces, and in assistance to the underdeveloped world.

Now, we can't force them to do it. We can't say, "Well, if you won't do it, we are going to withdraw our forces and leave Europe naked." But I think the United States has done pretty well in carrying its burdens, and we hope that Western Europe, now that it is prosperous, will do its part. We put $12 billion in Western Europe in four years, from 1948 to 1952. The amount of assistance we have given Latin America for the Alliance for Progress is a fraction of that.

So we have a right, it seems to me, as we have done and proven that we are not sunshine soldiers with respect to Europe itself; there isn't a country in Europe that is putting, of the countries that we are talking about, that is putting as many men and as large a proportion of its population and its gross national product into defence as we are.

We today pay 30 per cent of the infrastructure costs of NATO, the supply lines to the depots in Europe. It costs us about $3 billion in our balance of payments. The aid we give around the world is—you know, the American people are very critical, and the American Press prints a lot of bad news, because bad news is news and good news is not news, so they get an impression always that the United States is not doing its part. When I just think of what we have done for fifteen years, since 1945, the countries we have sustained, the alliances of which we are the whole, the centre, the willingness of the United States to accept burdens all around the world, I think it is a fantastic story.

We have one million Americans today serving outside the United States. There is no other country in history that has carried this kind of a burden. There are other countries who had forces serving outside of their own country but for conquest. We have two divisions in South Korea, not to control South Korea, but to defend it. We have a lot of Americans in South Vietnam. Well, now, no other country in the world has ever done that since the beginning of the world: Greece, Rome, Napoleon, and all the rest, always had conquest. We have a million men outside and they are trying to defend these countries. Now what we are saying is that rich Western Europe must do its part, and I hope it will.

I think Western Europe's success, after all, represents the greatest success of American foreign policy, since World War II, the rebuilding of Europe. It is just what we want. They are bound to have differences of opinion with us. But all we ask Western Europe to do is not look inward and just become a rich, careful secluded group, but to play their role in this great world struggle, as we have done it.

We don't want six or seven nuclear powers in Europe diverting their funds to nuclear power, when the United States has got this tremendous arsenal. But if these countries want to do it, we are not stopping them from doing it. If the French decide they want to become a nuclear power themselves, that is their decision. The question is whether the United States should join in helping make France a nuclear power, then Italy, then West Germany, then Belgium. How does that produce security when you have ten, twenty, thirty nuclear powers who may fire their weapons off under different conditions? That isn't in our interest, or in my opinion in the interest of peace, or the interest of Western Europe. And it is awfully expensive. Why duplicate what we have already done, and are doing in Western Europe today, as long as our guarantees are good?

FROM PRESIDENT KENNEDY'S REMARKS AT NATO HEADQUARTERS IN NAPLES

July 2nd, 1963

I shall return to Washington newly confirmed in my convictions regarding eight principal propositions:

First: It is increasingly clear that our Western European Allies are committed to the path of progressive democracy—to social justice and economic reform attained through the free processes of debate and consent. I spoke of this last night in Rome, as I had earlier spoken of it in Germany. And I cite it again here to stress the fact that this is not a matter of domestic politics but a key to Western freedom and solidarity. Nations which agree in applying at home the principles of freedom and justice are better able to understand each other and work together in world affairs.

And the more the nations of Western Europe commit themselves to democratic progress in their own countries, the more likely they are to co-operate sincerely in the construction of the emerging European community.

Second: It is increasingly clear that our Western European Allies are determined to maintain and co-ordinate their military strength in co-operation with my own nation. In a series of military briefings and reviews, I have been impressed, less by NATO's weaknesses, which are so often discussed, and more by the quality of the men, their officers, their steadily more modern weapons, their command structure, and their dedication to freedom and peace.

Since 1955, NATO's strength has greatly increased.

Third: It is increasingly clear that our Western European Allies are committed to peace. The purpose of our military strength is peace. The purpose of our partnership is peace. So our negotiations for an end to nuclear tests and our opposition to nuclear dispersal are fully consistent with our attention to defence—these are all complementary parts of a single strategy for peace.

We do not believe that war is unavoidable or that negotiations are inherently undesirable. We do believe that an end to the arms race is in the interest of all and that we can move toward that end with injury to none.

In negotiations to achieve peace, as well as preparation to prevent war, the West is united, and no Ally will abandon the interests of another to achieve a spurious détente. But, as we are to parley, we will not reject any path or refuse any proposal without examining its possibilities for peace.

Fourth: It is increasingly clear that our Western European Allies are willing to look outward on the world, not merely in at their own needs and demands. The economic institutions and support of Western European unity are founded on the principles of co-operation, not isolation, on expansion, not restriction.

The Common Market was not designed by its founders, and encouraged by the United States, to build walls against other Western countries—or to build walls against the ferment and hope of the developing nations. These nations need assistance in their struggle for political and economic independence. They need markets for their products and capital for their economies.

Our Allies in Europe, I am confident, will increase their role in this all-important effort—not only in lands with which they were previously associated but in Latin America and every area of need.

Fifth: It is increasingly clear that nations united in freedom are better able to build their economies than those that are repressed by tyranny. In the last ten years, the gross national product of the NATO nations has risen by some 75 per cent. We can do better than we are—but we are doing better than the party dictatorships to the East.

There was a time when some would say that this system of admitted dictatorship, for all its political and social faults, for all its denials of personal liberty, nevertheless seemed to offer a successful economic system—a swift and certain path to modernisation, growth and prosperity.

But it is now apparent that this system is incapable in to-day's world of achieving the organisation of agriculture, the satisfying of consumer demands, and the attainment of lasting prosperity. You only need to compare West Berlin with East Berlin; West Germany with East Germany; Western Europe with Eastern Europe.

Communism has sometimes succeeded as a scavenger but never a leader. It has never come to power in any country that was not disrupted by war, internal repression or both. Rejecting reform and diversity in freedom, the Communists cannot reconcile their ambitions for domination with other men's ambition for freedom.

They cannot look with confidence on a world of diversity and free choice, where order replaces chaos and progress drives out poverty. The increasing strains appearing within this once monolithic bloc—intellectual, economic, ideological and agricultural—made it increasingly clear that this system, with all its repression, is outmoded and doomed to failure.

Sixth: It is increasingly clear that the people of Western Europe are moved by a strong and irresistible desire for unity. Whatever path is chosen, whatever delays or obstacles are encountered, that movement will go forward; and the United States welcomes this movement and the greater strength it ensures.

We did not assist in the revival of Europe to maintain its dependence on the United States; nor do we seek to bargain selectively with many and separate voices.

We welcome a stronger partner. For today no nation can build its destiny alone; the age of self-sufficient nationalism is over. The age of interdependence is here.

The cause of Western European unity is based on logic and common sense. It is based on moral and political truths. It is based on sound military and economic principles. And it is based on the tide of history.

Seventh: It is increasingly clear that the United States and Western Europe are tightly bound by shared goals and mutual respect. On both sides of the Atlantic, trade barriers are being reduced, military co-operation is increasing, and the cause of Atlantic unity is being promoted.

There will always be honest differences among friends; and they should be freely and frankly discussed. But these are differences of means, not ends. They are differences of approach, not spirit.

Eighth, and finally: It is increasingly clear—and increasingly understood—that the central moving force of our great adventure is enduring mutual trust.

I came to Europe to reassert—as clearly and persuasively as I could—that the American commitment to the freedom of Europe is reliable—not merely because of good will, though that is strong—not merely because of a shared heritage, though that is deep and wide—and not at all because we seek to dominate; we do not.

I came to make it clear that this commitment rests upon the inescapable requirements of intelligent self-interest—it is a commitment whose wisdom is confirmed both by its absence when two great wars began and by its presence in eighteen years of well-defended peace.

The response which this message has evoked—from European citizens, from the Press, and from leaders of the Continent—makes it increasingly clear that our commitment—and its durability—are understood.

And at the same time, all that I have seen and heard in these ten crowded days confirms me in the conviction—which I am proud to proclaim to my own countrymen—

that the free men and free governments of free Europe are also firm in their commitment to our common cause.

One hundred and fifteen years ago this month, Giuseppe Mazzini addressed a mass meeting in Milan with these words:

"We are here... to build up the unity of the human family, so that the day may come when it shall represent a single sheepfold with a single shepherd—the spirit of God. Beyond the Alps, beyond the sea, are other peoples now . . . striving by different routes to reach the same goal—improvement, association and the foundation of an authority that shall put an end to world anarchy . . . united with them —they will unite with you."

Today, Italy is united as a free nation and committed to unity abroad. And beyond the Alps in the capitals of Western Europe, beyond the sea in the capitals of North America, other nations and other peoples are also striving for new association and improvement.

By building Western unity, we are ending the sources of discord that have so often produced war in the past—and we are strengthening the ties of solidarity that can deter further wars in the future.

In time, therefore, the unity of the West can lead to the unity of East and West, until the human family is truly a "single sheepfold" under God.

FROM PRESIDENT KENNEDY'S ADDRESS AT BERLIN CITY HALL

June 26th, 1963

I am proud to come to this city as the guest of your distinguished Mayor, who has symbolised throughout the world the fighting spirit of West Berlin. And I am proud to visit the Federal Republic with your distinguished Chancellor, who for so many years has committed Germany to democracy and freedom and progress—and to come here in the company of my fellow American, General Clay, who has been in this city during its great moments of crisis and will come again if ever needed.

Two thousand years ago, the proudest boast was: "Civis Romanus sum" (I am a Roman citizen). Today, in the world of freedom, the proudest boast is: "Ich bin ein Berliner" (I am a Berliner).

There are many people in the world who really don't understand—or say they don't—what is the great issue between the free world and the Communist world. Let them come to Berlin.

There are some who say that Communism is the wave of the future. Let them come to Berlin.

And there are some who say—in Europe and elsewhere—we can work with the Communists. Let them come to Berlin.

And there are even a few who say that it's true that Communism is an evil system, but it permits us to make economic progress. Lass sie nach Berlin kommen. (Let them come to Berlin.)

Freedom has many difficulties, and democracy is not perfect. But we have never had to put a wall up to keep our people in—to keep them from leaving us.

I want to say on behalf of my countrymen, who live many miles away on the other side of the Atlantic—who are far distant from you—that they take the greatest pride that they have been able to share with you, even from a distance, the story of the last eighteen years. I know of no town, no city that has been besieged for eighteen years that still lives with the vitality, and the force, and the hope, and the determination of the city of West Berlin.

While the wall is the most obvious and vivid demonstration of the failures of the Communist system for all the world to see, we take no satisfaction in it. For it is, as your Mayor said, an offence not only against history, but an offence against humanity—separating families, dividing husbands and wives and brothers and sisters, and dividing up people who wish to be joined together.

What is true of this city is true of Germany. Real lasting peace in Europe can never be assured as long as one German out of four is denied the elementary right of free men, and that is to make a free choice. In eighteen years of peace and good faith, this generation of Germans has earned the right to be free, including the right to unite their families and their nation in lasting peace with good will to all people.

You live in a defended island of freedom. But your life is part of the main. So let me ask you as I close to lift your eyes beyond the dangers of today to the hope of tomorrow—beyond the freedom merely of this city of Berlin, or your country of Germany—to the advance of freedom everywhere; beyond the wall, to the day of peace with justice; beyond yourselves, and ourselves, to all mankind.

Freedom is indivisible. And when one man is enslaved, all are not free. When all are free, then we can look forward to that day when this city will be joined as one—and this country and this great continent of Europe—in a peaceful and hopeful globe.

When that day finally comes—as it will—the people of West Berlin can take sober satisfaction in the fact that they were in the front lines for almost two decades.

All free men, wherever they may be, are citizens of Berlin. Therefore, as a free man, I take pride in the words: "Ich bin ein Berliner."

Kennedy and Europe

Like his predecessor, President Eisenhower, John Fitzgerald Kennedy brought the prestige of his office and the full weight of his forceful personality to bear on matters of foreign policy. Four months after his Inauguration he made his first journey to Europe. He chose to begin with France, his choice being dictated partly by the importance of the role which he hoped France would play in the "Grand Design" and partly for personal reasons of historic sentiment. The President and Mrs. Kennedy stayed in Paris from May 31st to June 3rd, 1961. Yet despite their enthusiastic reception, no mutual feeling of genuine confidence and understanding was to emerge between Kennedy and de Gaulle.

His next objective was to make the personal acquaintance of his chief rival, Nikita Khrushchev. The two men met on June 4th in Vienna. Kennedy was determined, above all, to convince the Soviet leader of the firm resolve of the United States to defend the peace, and to warn him of the dangers of miscalculation. The very opposite occurred. Khrushchev presented new demands over Berlin and went away with the definite impression that Kennedy was uncertain and irresolute.

On his way home, having summed up the situation in Europe, Kennedy paid a call on the British Prime Minister, Mr. Macmillan. Much more significant, however, was the later meeting between the two men at Nassau in the Bahamas in December 1962. Its chief purpose was to try to avert a crisis in Anglo-American relations and to set up a common nuclear strategy for the Western alliance. The difficulties were played down but not resolved, and the outcome of the meeting strengthened President de Gaulle in his determination to prevent the United Kingdom from becoming a member of the European Common Market.

The second European visit was much more successful. It was, however, to be John F. Kennedy's last major essay in foreign affairs. This time, for urgent political reasons, he chose the German Federal Republic as his first port of call. On June 23rd, 1963, he was warmly received in Bonn. The most important features of the visit, however, were the forthright speeches he delivered in Frankfurt's Paulskirche and in West Berlin, both of which were well received.

After this Kennedy paid a happy and most moving visit to Ireland, his family's native land, and this was followed by a conference in London. Next he went on to make a State visit to Italy, including an audience with the Pope, and ending with a speech in Naples at the Southern headquarters of NATO.

While Kennedy was President, many foreign Heads of State and innumerable high dignitaries and officials from all parts of the world were received at the White House. Among them were Macmillan, Adenauer, Nehru, Ikeda and Ben Bella. None of these eminent visitors went away without being profoundly impressed by the young President's remarkable abilities, and each of them took away something of lasting value from his White House discussions.

Kennedy brought to the White House setting a warmth and a brilliance which had only been very rarely encountered under previous administrations. Representatives of the arts and sciences were freely welcomed, and in this atmosphere of hospitality Kennedy's charming wife Jacqueline played her own important part. But the chief and special features that impressed and delighted his visitors, both friends and opponents, were the rare quality of Kennedy's mind, his keen, questing intelligence, his lively conversation and the force of his engaging personality.

In connection with the "Alianza para el progreso", a programme of economic support for Latin America announced during the early days of his Administration, which he hoped would have similar effects to the Marshall Plan in Europe, President Kennedy visited Columbia and Venezuela in December 1961. Unlike a previous traveller, former Vice-President Nixon, Kennedy's welcome was spontaneous and warmhearted.

Paris

On his first European trip as President, Kennedy chose Paris for his first stop. With police and army units in full force, the landing at Orly Airport on May 31st, 1961, was a grand affair. Eager to make a lasting impression on the young President, French President de Gaulle presided at dinner in the Hall of Mirrors at Versailles and was host for a gala at the Opéra. Kennedy's impression on the Parisians was no less meaningful and he won their hearts with his opening remarks to the assembled press, "I do not think it altogether inappropriate to introduce myself to this audience. I am the man who accompanied Jacqueline Kennedy to Paris." But Kennedy had not come to Europe to be impressed and to exchange polite words. In his address to the American public after his return he said: "This was not a ceremonial trip. Two aims of American foreign policy, above all others, were the reason for the trip: the unity of the free world, whose strength is the security of us all, and the eventual achievement of a lasting peace. My trip was devoted to the advancement of these two aims. My talks with General de Gaulle were profoundly encouraging to me. Certain differences in our attitudes on one or another problem became insignificant in view of our common commitment to defend freedom. The conclusions that we reached will be important for the future—in our agreement on defending Berlin, on working to improve the defences of Europe, to aiding the economic and political independence of the underdeveloped world, including Latin America, on spurring European economic unity, on concluding successfully the conference on Laos, and on closer consultations and solidarity in the Western Alliance." These words were spoken during the early days of his Presidency. Events changed the direction of policies. President de Gaulle wanted to go his own way. On his second trip to Europe, in the summer of 1963, President Kennedy pointedly avoided a second visit to Paris.

Pages 90—91:
Parisians cheer the President and Jacqueline Kennedy on the way from Orly Airport to the Quai d'Orsay where they were to stay during their visit to Paris.

Pages 92—93:
President Kennedy and his wife Jacqueline with President and Madame de Gaulle in the President's box at the Opéra.

President Kennedy
talking to President
de Gaulle.

Vienna

On June 3rd, 1961, President Kennedy flew from Paris to Vienna. He met the Russian Prime Minister, Mr. Khrushchev, for a number of talks, first in the American Embassy and later in the Russian Embassy (pages 96—97). The talks were to help Kennedy to evaluate the problems of co-existence with the Communist bloc and to explore new approaches towards ending the cold war. Here Kennedy arrives at Vienna Airport where he is met by Dr. Adolf Schaerf, President of the Austrian Republic.

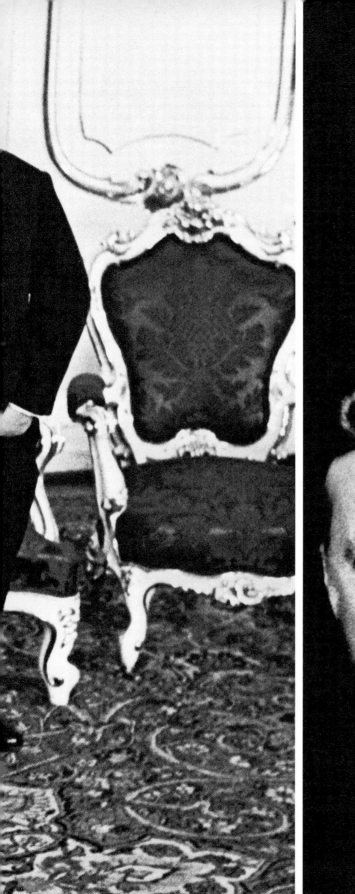

We have wholly different views of right and wrong, of what is an internal affair and what is aggression, and, above all, we have wholly different concepts of where the world is and where it is going. We believe in a system of national freedom and independence. He believes in an expanding and dynamic concept of world Communism.

The Vienna talks demonstrated how much work we in the free world have to do and how long and hard a struggle must be our faith as Americans in this generation as the chief defenders of the cause of liberty.

On the evening of June 3rd Kennedy and Khrushchev were guests of Dr. Schaerf, President of the Austrian Republic, at a dinner party at Schloss Schoenbrunn. Left to right: Khrushchev, Jacqueline Kennedy, Dr. Schaerf, Nina Khrushcheva, Kennedy.

London

To those old Allies whose cultural and spiritual origins we share, we pledge the loyalty of faithful friends. United, there is little we cannot do in a host of new cooperative ventures.

London was the only city visited more than once by Kennedy while he was in office and no closer contact existed with any head of government than the one between the President and Prime Minister Macmillan. Early in 1961 Macmillan had been Kennedy's guest for talks in Washington and aboard the Presidential yacht "Honey Fitz". At the close of this first trip he visited London on personal matters but made use of the occasion to discuss with Prime Minister Macmillan the impressions he had received in Paris and Vienna.

Later, the two statesmen met on a number of occasions in Washington and once in Nassau. Despite their differences, they were united on the need for Anglo-American unity and a common defence policy through NATO. The desire for economic unity throughout Europe and the search for solutions to world problems led to a strong mutual feeling of respect and admiration.

At the end of June 1963, when President Kennedy finished his visit to the Kennedy family's ancestral home in Ireland, he journeyed with the Prime Minister to Macmillan's country home, Birch Grove, Sussex, where they held two days of conferences.

From 26th to 29th June 1963, Kennedy visited Ireland, and on June 28th he made a speech before the Irish Parliament, in which he said: "I am proud to be the first American President to visit Ireland during his term of office, proud to be addressing this distinguished assembly, and proud of the welcome you have given me. It matters not how small a nation is that seeks world peace and freedom, for, to paraphrase a citizen of my country: 'The humblest nation of all the world, when clad in the armour of a righteous cause, is stronger than all the hosts of error.'"

President Kennedy visited Prime Minister Macmillan at Birch Grove on June 29th. Between talks the Prime Minister showed his guest over the estate.

On the occasion of their first visit to Great Britain in 1961, John and Jacqueline Kennedy were guests of the Queen.

During his second trip to Europe in the summer of 1963, the President visited Ireland and went to New Ross. He paid a visit to the birthplace of his ancestors, an old farm house. Mary Ryan, née Kennedy, gave him a warm welcome, and the Irish claimed him as a true son of Ireland.

Italy

On July 2nd, 1963, President Kennedy arrived at Rome, where he conferred with Signor Segni, Prime Minister Leone, Foreign Minister Piccioni, and other personalities. On July 3rd President Kennedy was received in audience by Pope Paul VI.

The people of Rome, used to visitors of high rank, simply watched President Kennedy drive through their city. In Naples, however, Kennedy's last stop before returning to the States, he was welcomed by enthusiastic crowds.

Germany

On June 23rd, 1963, Preside[n]
Kennedy started his visit [to]
Germany, a personal trium[ph]
from beginning to end. H[is]
visits to Bonn, Colog[ne]
Frankfurt, Wiesbaden a[nd]
Berlin convinced Germany [of]
the United States' will to [de]
fend the free world.
President Kennedy arrives [at]
Bonn. The President a[nd]
Chancellor Adenauer stand [at]
attention as the band of [the]
Bundeswehr plays the t[wo]
national anthems.
At Wahn Airport Preside[nt]
Kennedy inspects the gua[rd]
of honour of the Bundeswe[hr]
Later Kennedy and Chanc[el]
lor Adenauer passed throu[gh]
Cologne, Bonn, and Bad C[o]
desberg, amid enthusias[tic]
crowds.

War in Europe, as we learned twice in forty years, destroys peace in America. A threat to the freedom of Europe is a threat to the freedom of America. That is why no administration in Washington can fail to respond to such a threat—not merely from goodwill but from necessity.

For we know now that freedom is more than the rejection of tyranny—that prosperity is more than an escape from want—that partnership is more than a sharing of power. These are all,

above all, great human adventures. They must have meaning and conviction and purpose—and because they do, in your country, and in mine, in all the nations of the Alliance, we are called to a great new mission.

We look forward to a Europe united and strong—speaking with a common voice—acting with a common will—a world power capable of meeting world problems as a full and equal partner.

On his visit to Germany, President Kennedy stopped at Cologne and Bonn, where he delivered public addresses. At Bad Godesberg Kennedy made a speech to the personnel of the U.S. Embassy. In the evening President Kennedy was guest of honour at a banquet and reception given by Chancellor Adenauer.

President Kennedy made the most important of his speeches on June 25th in Frankfurt's Paulskirche. He promised to maintain freedom and to adhere resolutely to the Atlantic partnership. Moreover, Kennedy assured the Germans that an attack upon Germany would be treated as an attack upon the U.S.

On June 23rd President Kennedy and Chancellor Adenauer went to Mass. Here the President leaves Cologne Cathedral.

President Kennedy talking with former Vice-Chancellor Erhard.

On the occasion of the reception given by President Heinrich Lübke in honour of the American President in the "Villa Hammerschmidt", the German equivalent of the American Peace Corps was founded. During the ceremony two small girls succeeded in slipping through the cordon of police and greeting the President.

President Kennedy bidding farewell to Germany.

In his Inaugural speech on January 20th, 1961, President Kennedy said: "To our sister republics, south of our border, we offer a special pledge—to convert our good words into good deeds—in a new alliance for progress—to assist free men and free governments in casting off the chains of poverty." In November 1961, Kennedy visited South America to further his Alliance for Progress scheme. Here he is seen greeting a party of workers in Venezuela.

Let every nation know, whether it wishes us well or ill, that we shall pay any price, bear any burden, meet any hardship, support any friend or oppose any foe to assure the survival and success of liberty.

In May of 1961, sent by Kennedy, Vice-President Johnson journeyed for a first-hand examination of the political situation in South and South-East Asia. In the province of Bien Hao in Vietnam, where Vice-President Johnson inquired about the success of the American aid programme, children with American flags welcome the visitor.

Since the first days of his Presidency, Kennedy had tried to settle the conflict in Laos. The United States endeavoured to strengthen and to neutralise this country, but the problem remains. Nevertheless John F. Kennedy's words still carry weight: "To those new States whom we welcome to the ranks of the free, we pledge our word that one form of colonial control shall not have passed away merely to be replaced by a far more iron tyranny. But we shall always hope to find them strongly supporting their own freedom—and to remember that, in the past, those who foolishly sought power by riding the back of the tiger ended up inside."

President Kennedy was untiring in his efforts to ease tension between West and East and to stop nuclear tests, as a first step towards greater security and lasting peace. On October 7th, 1963, he had the great satisfaction of signing the treaty on banning nuclear tests in the atmosphere. The scene is the White House; next to Kennedy are members of the U.S. Congress. This was to be the last important political act of the President.

There was scarcely a month without foreign statesmen and dignitaries visiting President Kennedy at Washington, an indication of the powerful impression he had already made on world politics as the true leader of the free world during the thousand days of his Presidency.

The Shah and Empress Farah Dibah of Iran visiting Washington. They were greeted by President Kennedy and his wife at the airport.

Mayor Willy Brandt as a guest at the White House.

One of the first European statesmen to visit President Kennedy was Chancellor Konrad Adenauer. During his stay at Washington he also made friends with John Jr.

In November 1961, Prime Minister Nehru came to the U.S. Here he is seen on his way to the White House together with Jacqueline Kennedy.

To that world assembly of sovereign States, the United Nations, we renew our pledge of support—to prevent it from becoming merely a forum for invective—to strengthen its shield of the new and the weak—and to enlarge the area in which its writ may run.

President Kennedy addressing the plenary session of U.N.O.

PRESIDENT KENNEDY'S SPEECH AT
ST. PAUL'S CATHEDRAL IN FRANKFURT

June 25th, 1963

One hundred and fifteen years ago a most learned Parliament was convened in this historic hall. Its goal was a united German Federation. Its members were poets and professors, lawyers and philosophers, doctors and clergymen, freely elected in all parts of the land. No nation applauded its endeavours as warmly as my own. No assembly ever strove more ardently to put perfection into practice. And though in the end it failed, no other building in Germany deserves more the title of "cradle of German democracy".

But can there be such a title? In my own home city of Boston, Faneuil Hall—once the meeting-place of the authors of the American Revolution—has long been known as the "cradle of American liberty". But when, in 1852, the Hungarian patriot Kossuth addressed an audience there, he criticized its name. "It is," he said, "a great name—but there is something in it which saddens my heart. You should not say 'American liberty'. You should say 'liberty in America'. Liberty should not be either American or European—it should just be 'liberty'."

Kossuth was right. For unless liberty flourishes in all lands, it cannot flourish in one. Conceived in one hall, it must be carried out in many. Thus the seeds of the American Revolution had been brought earlier from Europe, and they later took root around the world. And the German Revolution of 1848 transmitted ideas and idealists to America and to other lands. Today, in 1963, democracy and liberty are more international than ever before. And the spirit of the Frankfurt Assembly, like the spirit of Faneuil Hall, must live in many hearts and nations if it is to live at all.

We are partners for peace, not in a narrow bilateral context, but in a framework of Atlantic Partnership. The ocean divides us less than the Mediterranean divided the ancient world of Greece and Rome. Our Constitution is old and yours is young—and our culture is young and yours is old—but in our commitment we can and must speak and act with but one voice. Our roles are distinct but complementary—and our goals are the same: Peace and freedom for all men, for all time, in a world of abundance, in a world of justice.

That is why our nations are working together to strengthen NATO, to expand trade, to assist the developing countries, to align our monetary policies and to build the Atlantic Community. I would not diminish the miracle of West Germany's economic achievements. But the true German miracle has been your rejection of the past for the future—your reconciliation with France, your participation in the building of Europe, your leading role in NATO, and your growing support for constructive undertakings throughout the world.

The future of the West lies in Atlantic Partnership—a system of co-operation, interdependence and harmony whose peoples can jointly meet their burdens and opportunities throughout the world. Some say this is only a dream, but I do not agree. A generation of achievement—the Marshall Plan, NATO, the Schuman Plan, and the Common Market—urges us up the path to greater unity.

Some say that the United States will neither hold to these purposes nor abide by its pledges—that we will revert to a narrow nationalism. But such doubts fly in the face of history. For eighteen years the United States has stood its watch for freedom all around the globe. The firmness of American will, and the effectiveness of American strength, have been shown in support of free men and free governments, in Asia, in Africa, in the Americas, and above all, here in Europe we have undertaken, and sustained in honour, relations of mutual trust and obligation with more than forty allies. We are proud of this record, which more than answers doubts. But, in addition, these proven commitments to the common freedom and safety are assured, in the future as in the past, by one great fundamental fact—that they are deeply rooted in America's own self-interest. Our commitment to Europe is indispensable—in our interest as well as yours.

It is not in our interest to try to dominate the European councils of decision. If that were our objective, we would prefer to see Europe divided and weak, enabling the United States to deal with each fragment individually. Instead we have and now look forward to a Europe united and strong—speaking with a common voice—acting with a common will—a world power capable of meeting world problems as a full and equal partner.

This is in the interest of us all. For War in Europe, as we learned twice in forty years, destroys peace in America. A threat to the freedom of Europe is a threat to the freedom of America. That is why no administration—no administration—in Washington can fail to respond to such a threat—not merely from goodwill but from necessity. And that is why we look forward to a united Europe in an Atlantic Partnership

—an entity of interdependent parts, sharing equally both burdens and decisions, and linked together in the task of defence as well as the arts of peace.

This is no fantasy. It will be achieved by concrete steps to solve the problems that face us all: military, economic and political. Partnership is not a posture but a process—a continuous process that grows stronger each year as we devote ourselves to common tasks.

The first task of the Atlantic Community was to assure its common defence. That defence was and still is indivisible. The United States will risk its cities to defend yours because we need your freedom to protect ours. Hundreds of thousands of our soldiers serve with yours on this continent, as tangible evidence of that pledge. Those who would doubt our pledge or deny this indivisibility—those who would separate Europe from America or split one Ally from another—would only give aid and comfort to the men who make themselves our adversaries and welcome any Western disarray.

The purpose of our common military effort is not war but peace—not the destruction of nations but the protection of freedom. The forces that West Germany contributes to this effort are second to none among the Western European nations. Your nation is in the front line of defence—and your divisions, side by side with our own, are a source of strength to us all.

These conventional forces are essential, and they are backed by the sanction of thousands of the most modern weapons here on European soil and thousands more, only minutes away, in posts around the world. Together our nations have developed for the forward defence of free Europe a deterrent far surpassing the present or prospective force of any hostile power.

Nevertheless, it is natural that America's nuclear position has raised questions within the Alliance. I believe we must confront these questions—not by turning the clock backward to separate nuclear deterrents—but by developing a more closely unified Atlantic deterrent, with genuine European participation.

How this can best be done—and it is not easy—in some ways more difficult to split the atom physically—how this can best be done is now under discussion with those who may wish to join in this effort. The proposal before us is for a new Atlantic force. Such a force would bring strength instead of weakness, cohesion instead of division. It would belong to all members, not one, with all participating on a basis of full equality. And as Europe moves toward unity, its role and responsibility, here as elsewhere, would and must increase accordingly. Meanwhile, there is much to do. We must work more closely together on strategy, training and planning. European officers from NATO are being assigned to Strategic Air Command Headquarters in Omaha, Nebraska. Modern weapons are being deployed here in Western Europe. And America's strategic deterrent—the most powerful in history, will continue to be at the service of the whole Alliance.

Second: Our partnership is not military alone. Economic unity is also imperative—not only among the nations of Europe, but across the wide Atlantic.

Indeed, economic co-operation is needed throughout the entire free world. By opening our markets to the developing countries of Africa, Asia and Latin America, by contributing our capital and our skills, by stabilizing basic prices, we can help assure them of a favourable climate for freedom and growth.

Another great economic challenge is in the coming round of trade negotiations. Those deliberations are much more important than a technical discussion of trade and commerce. They are an opportunity to build common industrial and agricultural policies across the Atlantic. They are an opportunity to open up new sources of demand, to give new impetus to growth, and make more jobs and prosperity, for our expanding populations. They are an opportunity to recognize the trading needs and aspirations of other free world countries, including Japan.

We must not return to the nineteen-thirties when we exported to each other our own stagnation. We must not return to the discredited view that trade favours some nations at the expense of others. Let no one think that the United States—with only a fraction of its economy dependent on trade and only a small part of that with Western Europe—is seeking trade expansion in order to dump our goods on this continent.

Trade expansion will help us all. The experience of the Common Market—like the experience of the German Zollverein—shows an increased rise in business activity and general prosperity resulting for all participants in such trade agreements, with no member profiting at the expense of another. Together we have been partners in adversity—let us also be partners in prosperity.

Beyond development and trade is monetary policy. Here again our interests run together. Indeed there is no field in which the wider interest of all more clearly outweighs the narrow interest of one. We have lived by that principle, as bankers of freedom, for a generation. Now that other nations—including West Germany—have found new economic strength, it is time for common efforts here, too. The great free nations of the world must take control of their monetary problems if those problems are not to take control for us.

Yet the reunion of Europe, as Europeans shape it— bringing a permanent end to the civil wars that have repeatedly wracked the world—will continue to have the determined support of the United States. For that reunion is a necessary step in strengthening the community of freedom. It would strengthen our Alliance for its defence. And it would be in our national interest as well as yours.

It is only a fully cohesive Europe that can protect us all against fragmentation of the Alliance. Only such a Europe will permit full reciprocity of treatment across the ocean, in facing the Atlantic agenda. With only such a Europe can we have a full give-and-take between equals, an equal sharing of responsibilities, and an equal level of sacrifice. I repeat again—so that there may be no misunderstanding—the choice of paths to the unity of Europe is a choice which Europe must make. But as you continue this great effort, undeterred by either difficulty or delay, you should know that this new European greatness will be not an object of fear, but a source of strength, for the United States of America.

There are other political tasks before us. We must all learn to practise more completely the art of consultation on matters stretching well beyond immediate military and economic questions.

Together, for example, we must explore the possibilities of easing the tensions of the cold war and reducing the dangers of the arms race. Together we must work to strengthen the spirit of those Europeans who are now not free, to re-establish their old ties to freedom and the West, so that their desire for liberty and their sense of nationhood and their sense of belonging to the Western Community, will survive for future expression.

All of us in the West must be faithful to our conviction that peace in Europe can never be complete until everywhere in Europe, and that includes Germany, men can choose, in peace and freedom, how their countries shall be governed, and choose—without threat to any neighbour—reunification with their countrymen.

I preach no easy liberation and I make no empty promises but my countrymen since our country was founded, believe strongly in the proposition that all men shall be free and all free men shall have this right of choice.

As we look steadily eastward in the hope and purpose of new freedom, we must also look—and evermore closely—to our transatlantic ties. The Atlantic Community will not soon become a single overarching super-state. But practical steps toward stronger common purpose are well within our means. As we widen our common effort in defence, and our three-fold co-operation in economics, we shall inevitably strengthen our political ties as well. Just as your current efforts for unity in Europe will produce a stronger voice in the dialogue between us, so in America our current battle for the liberty and prosperity of all citizens can only deepen the meaning of our common historic purposes.

For we know now that freedom is more than the rejection of tyranny—that prosperity is more than an escape from want—that partnership is more than a sharing of power. These are all, above all, great human adventures. They must have meaning and conviction and purpose—and because they do, in your country, and in mine, in all the nations of the Alliance, we are called to a great new mission.

It is not a mission of self-defence alone—for that is a means, not an end. It is not a mission of arbitrary power—for we reject the idea that one nation should dominate another. Our mission is to create a new social order founded on liberty and justice, in which men are the masters of their fate, in which States are the servants of their citizens, and in which all men and women can share a better life for themselves and their children. That is the object of our common policy.

To realize this vision, we must seek above all, a world of peace—a world in which peoples dwell together in mutual respect and work together in mutual regard—a world where peace is not a mere interlude between wars, but an incentive to the creative energies of humanity. We will not find such a peace today, or even tomorrow. The obstacles to hope are large and menacing. Yet the goal of a peaceful world must—today and tomorrow—shape our decisions and inspire our purposes.

So we are all idealists. We are all visionaries. Let it not be said of this Atlantic generation that we left ideals and visions to the past, nor purpose and determination to our adversaries. We have come too far, we have sacrificed too much, to disdain the future now. And we shall ever remember what Goethe told us—that the "highest wisdom, the best that mankind ever knew" was the realization that "he only earns his freedom and existence who daily conquers them anew."

FROM PRESIDENT KENNEDY'S SPEECH
BEFORE U.N. GENERAL ASSEMBLY

September 20th, 1963

We meet again in the quest for peace.

Twenty-four months ago, when I last had the honour of addressing this body, the shadow of fear lay darkly across the world. The freedom of West Berlin was in immediate peril. Agreement on a neutral Laos seemed remote. The mandate of the U.N. in the Congo was under fire. The financial outlook for this organisation was in doubt. Dag Hammarskjold was dead. The doctrine of Troika was being pressed in his place and atmospheric nuclear tests had recently been resumed by the Soviet Union.

Today the clouds have lifted a little so that new rays of hope can break through. The pressures on West Berlin appear to be temporarily eased. Political unity in the Congo has been largely restored. A neutral coalition in Laos, while still in difficulty, is at least in being. The integrity of the U.N. Secretariat has been reaffirmed. A U.N. decade of development is under way. And, for the first time in seventeen years of effort, a specific step has been taken to limit the nuclear arms race.

I refer, of course, to the treaty to ban nuclear tests in the atmosphere, outer space and under water—concluded by the Soviet Union, the United Kingdom and the United States—and already signed by nearly a hundred countries.

Today we may have reached a pause in the cold war—but that is not a lasting peace. A test ban treaty is a milestone—but that is not the millennium. We have been given an opportunity. And if we fail to make the most of this moment and this momentum—if we convert our new-found hopes and understanding into new walls and weapons of hostility—if this pause in the cold war leads merely to its renewal and not its end—then the shaming indictment of posterity will rightly point its finger at us all.

But if we can stretch this into a period of fruitful co-operation—if both sides can now gain new confidence and true experience in concrete collaborations for peace—if we can now be as bold and far-sighted in the control of deadly weapons as we have been in their creation—then, surely, this first small step can be the start of a long and fruitful journey.

The task of building the peace lies with the leaders of every nation, large and small. For the great powers have no monopoly on conflict or ambition. The cold war is not the only expression of tension in this world—and the nuclear race is not the only arms race. Even little wars are dangerous in a nuclear world. The long labour of peace is an undertaking for all nations—and in this effort none of us can remain unaligned.

The reduction of global tension must not be an excuse for the narrow pursuit of self-interest. If the Soviet Union and the United States, with all their global interests and clashing commitments of ideology, and with nuclear weapons still aimed at each other, can find areas of common interest and agreement, then surely other nations can do the same—nations caught in regional conflicts, in racial issues, or in the death throes of the old colonialism.

The fact remains that the United States, as a major nuclear power, has a special responsibility. It is, in fact, a three-fold responsibility—a responsibility to our own citizens—a responsibility to the people of all the world affected by our decisions—and to the next generation of humanity. We believe the Soviet Union also has these special responsibilities —and that these responsibilities require our two countries to concentrate less on our differences and more on the means of resolving them peacefully.

Our conflicts, to be sure, are real. Our concepts of the world are different. No service is performed by failing to make clear our disagreements. A central difference is the belief of the American people in self-determination for all peoples.

We believe that the people of Germany and Berlin must be free to reunite their capital and their country.

We believe that the people of Cuba must be free to secure the fruits of the revolution that has been so falsely betrayed from within and exploited from without.

In short, we believe that in all the world—in Eastern Europe as well as Western, in Southern Africa as well as Northern, in old nations as well as new—people must be free to choose their own future, without discrimination or dictation, and without coercion or subversion.

But I would say to the leaders of the Soviet Union, and to their people, that if neither of our countries is to be fully secure, we need a much better weapon than the H-bomb— a weapon better than ballistic missiles or nuclear submarines —and that better weapon is peaceful co-operation.

We have, in recent years, agreed on a limited nuclear test ban treaty—on an emergency communications link between our capitals—on a statement of principles for disarmament

—on an increase in cultural exchange—on co-operation in outer space—on the peaceful exploration of the Antarctic—and on tempering last year's crisis over Cuba.

I believe, therefore, that the Soviet Union and the United States, together with their allies, can achieve further agreements—agreements which spring from our mutual interest in avoiding mutual destruction.

There can be no doubt about the agenda of further steps. We must continue to seek agreement on measures to prevent war by accident or miscalculation. We must continue to seek agreement on safeguards against surprise attack, including observation posts at key points. We must continue to seek agreement on further measures to curb the nuclear arms race, by controlling the transfer of nuclear weapons, converting fissionable materials to peaceful purposes, and banning underground testing with adequate inspection and enforcement. We must continue to seek agreement on a freer flow of information and people from East to West and West to East.

We must continue to seek agreement, encouraged by yesterday's affirmative response to this proposal by the Soviet Foreign Minister, on an arrangement to keep weapons of mass destruction out of outer space.

In these and other ways, let us move up the steep and difficult path toward comprehensive disarmament, securing mutual confidence through mutual verification, and building the institutions of peace as we dismantle the engines of war. We must not let failure to agree on all points delay agreement where agreement is possible. And we must not put forward proposals merely for propaganda purposes.

Finally, in a field where the United States and the Soviet Union have a special capacity—the field of space—there is room for new co-operation for further joint efforts in the regulation and exploration of space. Include among these possibilities a joint expedition to the moon. Space offers no problem of sovereignty; by resolution of this Assembly, the members of the United Nations have forsworn any claims to territorial rights in outer space or on celestial bodies, and declared that international law and the U.N. Charter will apply. Why, therefore, should man's first flight to the moon be a matter of national competition? Why should the United States and the Soviet Union, in preparing for such expeditions, become involved in immense duplications of research, construction and expenditure? Surely we should explore whether the scientists and astronauts of our two countries—indeed of all the world—cannot work together in the conquest of space, sending some day in this decade to the moon, not the representatives of a single nation, but the representatives of all humanity.

The contest will continue—the contest between those who envision a monolithic world and those who believe in diversity—but it should be a contest in leadership instead of destruction, a contest in achievement instead of intimidation. Speaking for the United States of America, I welcome such a contest. For we believe that truth is stronger than error—and that freedom is more enduring than coercion. And in the contest for a better life, all the world can be the winner.

The effort to improve the conditions of man, however, is not the task of a few. It is the task of all nations—acting alone, acting in groups and acting in the United Nations. For plague and pestilence, plunder and pollution, the hazards of nature and the hunger of children are the foes of every nation. The earth, the sea, and the air are the concern of every nation. And science, technology and education can be the allies of every nation.

Never before has man had such capacity to control his own environment—to end thirst and hunger—to conquer poverty and disease—to banish illiteracy and massive human misery. We have the power to make this the best generation of mankind in the history of the world—or to make it the last.

STATEMENT BY PRESIDENT KENNEDY ON THE DEATH OF MRS. ELEANOR ROOSEVELT

November 7th, 1962

One of the great ladies in the history of this country has passed from the scene. Her loss will be deeply felt by all those who admired her tireless idealism or benefited from her good works and wise counsel.

Since the day I entered this office, she has been both an inspiration and a friend, and my wife and I always looked forward to her visits to the White House, to which she always lent such grace and vitality.

Our condolences go to all the members of her family, whose grief at the death of this extraordinary woman can be tempered by the knowledge that her memory and spirit will long endure among those who labour for great causes around the world.

FROM THANKSGIVING DAY ADDRESS

November 22nd, 1962

It is fitting that we observe this year our own day of thanksgiving. It is fitting that we give our thanks for the safety of our land, for the fertility of our harvests, for the strength of our liberties, for the health of our people. We do so in no spirit of self-righteousness. We recognise that we are the beneficiaries of the toil and devotion of our fathers and that we can pass their legacy on to our children only by equal toil and equal devotion. We recognise, too, that we live in a world of peril and change—and in so uncertain a time we are all the more grateful for the indestructible gifts of hope and love, which sustain us.

Let us renew the spirit of the Pilgrims at the first Thanksgiving, lonely in an inscrutable wilderness.

Let us renew that spirit by preparing our souls for the incertitudes ahead—by being always ready to confront crisis with steadfastness and achievement with grace and modesty.

Personal Background

The Kennedys are a clan with close family links, a strong sense of purpose and a proud record of distinguished achievement in many fields. Though bound together by a common origin and a common faith, they are neither exclusive nor sectarian, and are bred in the tradition of public service.

John Fitzgerald Kennedy, the second son of Joseph P. Kennedy, was born at Brookline, Mass., a suburb of Boston, on May 29th, 1917. His mother, Rose, also of Irish extraction, was a noted beauty. His father had attended Harvard University and had then entered the business world, where he rapidly built up a considerable fortune. In 1932 he helped Franklin D. Roosevelt to become President, and under the banner of the New Deal assumed the chairmanship of the Securities and Exchange Commission, being instrumental in ushering in much needed reforms on the Stock Exchange. From 1937 until November 1940, he was United States Ambassador in London, and used all his influence to dissuade the United States from entering the war.

John (known in the family as Jack) Kennedy was at this time writing his first book *Why England Slept*, and shortly afterwards completed his studies at Harvard. In 1941 he joined the U.S. Navy. On the night of August 2nd, 1943, a Japanese destroyer rammed the motor torpedo-boat he was commanding, in Blackett Strait, off the Solomon Islands. Although wounded, the young commander saved all the members of his crew who had survived the collision. He was awarded high service decorations for his courageous conduct.

For each of his children—Joseph, John, Eunice, Patricia, Robert, Jean and Edward—Joseph Kennedy had made precise plans as regards education and future career.

The eldest son had been destined and prepared for politics, but when he was killed as a bomber pilot, the way was clear for John to follow his own expressed inclinations and talents for a political career.

On September 12th, 1953, already a U.S. Senator, John F. Kennedy married Jacqueline Lee Bouvier, the daughter of a New York banker, John Bouvier. She had enjoyed a comprehensive education at American colleges and at the Paris Sorbonne, and had then become a journalist and press photographer. In 1957 (after an earlier miscarriage) a daughter, Caroline Bouvier, was born, and in 1960 a son, John Fitzgerald. A second son died shortly after birth in 1963.

Brothers, sisters, brothers-in-law and sisters-in-law joined loyally in supporting and helping John Kennedy at every stage of his career, culminating in his rise to the Presidency. As President he was to entrust them with important tasks, knowing he could trust them completely to implement his plans.

Family Album

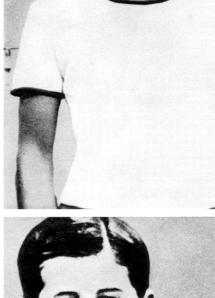

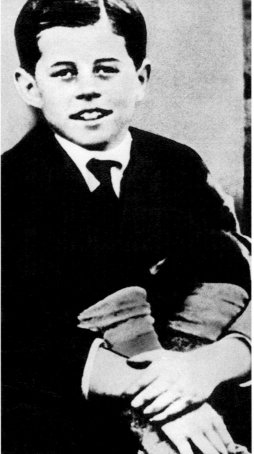

In 1938 John F. Kennedy was a member of the Harvard University swimming team. To the hard training he got there he would later owe his life in World War II.

In World War II John F. Kennedy served as a lieutenant in the U.S. Navy. In 1943 he was made commander of a torpedo boat operating in the Pacific.

Eight-year-old John F. Kennedy at Dexter School, Brookline.

Lieutenant junior grade John F. Kennedy commanded torpedo boat PT 109 in the Pacific in the summer of 1943. Operating against the Japanese, Kennedy's boat was cut in two by a Japanese destroyer on the night of August 2nd. Kennedy and the surviving crew members swam to safety. Kennedy pulled along one of his badly wounded men, tied to a line, the end of which he held between his teeth.

These pictures show Kennedy with his crew and steering his torpedo boat (above and right). Left: Kennedy receives the Navy and Marine Corps Medal.

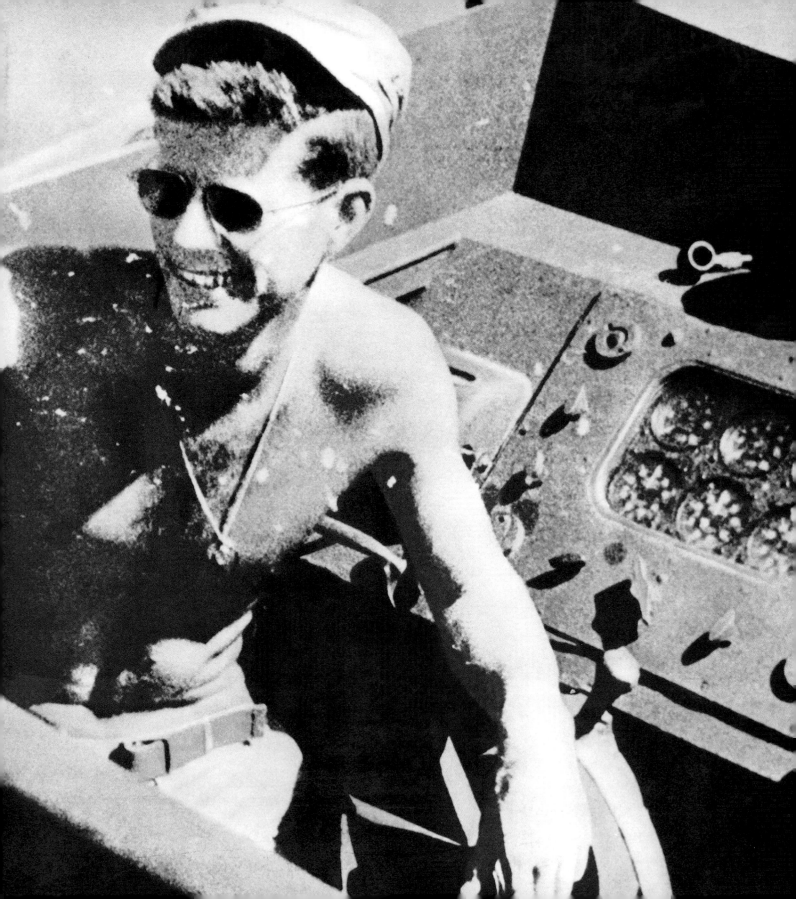

The Kennedy family in 1938. On the extreme left the father, Joseph P. Kennedy, the U.S. Ambassador to London; behind him John F. Kennedy. Extreme right: elder brother, Joseph P. Jr., killed when his plane exploded over Germany in World War II.

At Newport on September 12th, 1953, Senator John F. Kennedy was married to Jacqueline Lee Bouvier, daughter of New York banker John Bouvier. 900 guests had been invited to this wedding, and thousands of spectators tried to break through the cordon of police to congratulate the happy couple.

Left: President John F. Kennedy in the garden in front of the White House, on his way to a press conference.

Below: Jacqueline Kennedy taking out John Jr. in the park of the White House.

Left: Summer 1960. Senator John F. Kennedy, already nominated for the Presidency, with Jacqueline in their yacht "Victura".

Right: Like her husband, Jacqueline Kennedy loves outdoor life and she is a fine rider. With John Jr. in front of her and Caroline on her pony "Macaroni" she gives a riding lesson.

Below: The Presidency didn't allow John F. Kennedy much spare time. The more welcome, therefore, were the few hours he could spend in the privacy of his family. Here John, Jacqueline, and Caroline visit the Civil War battlefield at Gettysburg.

President Kennedy devoted the majority of his rare spare time to his family. The children became nation-wide favourites, and their frank remarks were often quoted in the press throughout the world.

These pictures found their way into the newspapers and magazines of the world. The President of the United States, the most powerful and at the same time the loneliest man in the world, is playing with his children. And every time John Jr. interfered with the rigid round of protocol, his father could hardly conceal his delight.

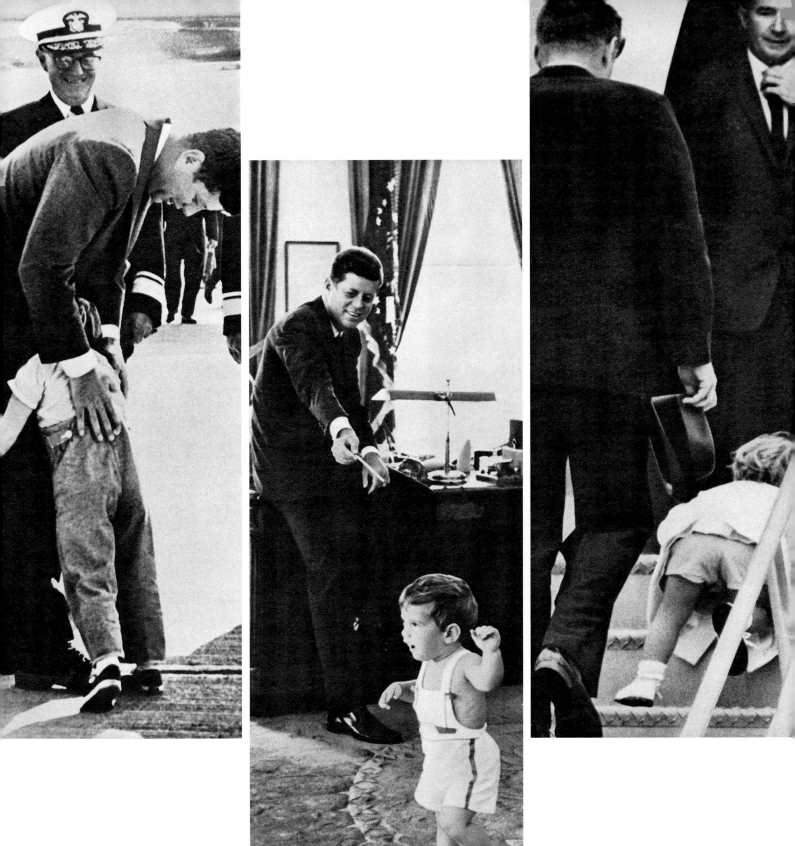

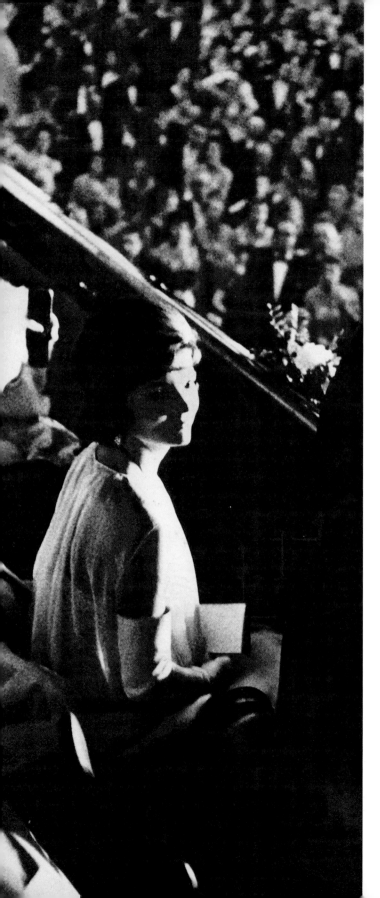

In Jacqueline Bouvier, the beautiful young wife of President Kennedy, were embodied all the characteristic qualities of her French ancestors. The formal and sedate atmosphere of the venerable official residence of the American President changed suddenly when Jacqueline entered the White House as First Lady of the United States. Her lively temperament and cheerfulness, her uncomplicated manners and aesthetic taste changed the look and spirit of the White House. Now scientists and artists, writers and actors began to mingle with the politicians at receptions and parties. Thanks to Jacqueline Kennedy the capital's social life acquired new splendour. Jacqueline's taste and style of living set the trend for the nation. Her beauty, her simplicity, and her charm gave the White House and the office of the Presidency a new warmth.

Left: The marked elegance of her wardrobe and the natural beauty of Jacqueline Kennedy were admired and imitated by hundreds of thousands of American women. — Jacqueline Kennedy at an inaugural dance in Washington.

Right: Jacqueline Kennedy remodelled the White House into a splendid home and a representative residence for the President of the United States. — Here the First Lady poses willingly and patiently for the photographers of the American press in the Blue Room, which she had redecorated.

Extreme right: On the second day after his Inauguration, President Kennedy played host to the late American Poet Laureate, Robert Frost, to thank him for reading one of his poems on the occasion of the Inaugural ceremony on the steps of the Capitol.

Receptions at the White House were designed by the President to inspire a wider interest and understanding of American artistic achievement. Here the President and Mrs. Kennedy receive writer Pearl S. Buck and poet Robert Frost, at a reception honouring America's Nobel Prize winners, who had assembled to listen to a concert by Pablo Casals. Said Kennedy in a toast the dinner, "I think this is the most extraordinary collectic of talent, of human knowledge, that has ever been gathered t gether at the White House, with the possible exception of wh Thomas Jefferson dined alone."

PRESIDENT KENNEDY'S ADDRESS TO THE NATION ON THE MILITARY BUILD-UP IN CUBA

October 22nd, 1962

This Government, as promised, has maintained the closest surveillance of the Soviet military build-up on the island of Cuba. Within the past week, unmistakable evidence has established the fact that a series of offensive missile sites is now in preparation on that imprisoned island. The purpose of these bases can be none other than to provide a nuclear strike capability against the Western hemisphere.

Upon receiving the first preliminary hard information of this nature last Tuesday morning at 9 a.m., I directed that our surveillance be stepped up. And having now confirmed and completed our evaluation of the evidence and our decision on a course of action, this Government feels obliged to report this new crisis to you in full detail.

The characteristics of these new missile sites indicate two distinct types of installations. Several of them include medium-range ballistic missiles, capable of carrying a nuclear warhead for a distance of more than 1,000 nautical miles. Each of these missiles, in short, is capable of striking Washington, D.C., the Panama Canal, Cape Canaveral, Mexico City, or any other city in the Eastern part of the United States, in Central America or in the Caribbean area.

Additional sites not yet completed appear to be designed for intermediate-range ballistic missiles—capable of travelling more than twice as far—and thus capable of striking most of the major cities in the Western hemisphere, ranging as far North as Hudson's Bay, Canada, and as far South as Lima, Peru. In addition, jet bombers, capable of carrying nuclear weapons, are now being uncrated and assembled on Cuba, while the necessary air bases are being prepared.

This urgent transformation of Cuba into an important strategic base—by the presence of these large, long-range and clearly offensive weapons of sudden mass destruction—constitutes an explicit threat to the peace and security of all the Americas, in flagrant and deliberate defiance of the Rio Pact of 1947, the traditions of this nation and hemisphere, the joint resolution of the 87th Congress, the Charter of the United Nations, and my own public warnings to the Soviets on September 4th and 13th. This action also contradicts the repeated assurances of Soviet spokesmen, both publicly and privately delivered, that the arms build-up in Cuba would retain its original defensive character, and that the Soviet Union had no need or desire to station strategic missiles on the territory of any other nation.

The size of this undertaking makes clear that it had been planned some months ago. Yet only last month, after I had made clear the distinction between any introduction of ground-to-ground missiles and the existence of defensive anti-aircraft missiles, the Soviet Government publicly stated on September 11th that "the armaments and military equipment sent to Cuba are designed exclusively for defensive purposes", that "there is no need for the Soviet Union to shift its weapons . . . for a retaliatory blow to any other country, for instance Cuba," and that "the Soviet Union has so powerful rockets to carry these nuclear warheads that there is no need to search for sites for them beyond the boundaries of the Soviet Union." That statement was false.

Only last Thursday, as evidence of this rapid offensive build-up was already in my hand, Soviet Foreign Minister Gromyko told me in my office that he was instructed to make it clear once again, as he said his Government had already done, that Soviet assistance to Cuba "pursued solely the purpose of contributing to the defence capabilities of Cuba," that "training by Soviet specialists of Cuban nationals in handling defensive armaments was by no means offensive," and that "if it were otherwise, the Soviet Government would never become involved in rendering such assistance." That statement also was false.

Neither the United States of America nor the world community of nations can tolerate deliberate deception and offensive threats on the part of any nation, large or small. We no longer live in a world where only the actual firing of weapons represents a sufficient challenge to a nation's security to constitute a maximum peril. Nuclear weapons are so destructive, and ballistic missiles are so swift, that any substantially increased possibility of their use or any sudden change in their deployment may well be regarded as a definite threat to the peace.

For many years, both the Soviet Union and the United States—recognising this fact—have deployed strategic nuclear weapons with great care, never upsetting the precarious status quo which ensured that these weapons would not be used in the absence of some vital challenge. Our own strategic missiles have never been transferred to the territory of any other nation under a cloak of secrecy and deception; and our history—unlike that of the Soviets since World War II—demonstrates that we have no desire to dominate or conquer any other nation or impose our system upon its people.

Nevertheless, American citizens have become adjusted to living daily on the bull's eye of Soviet missiles located inside the U.S.S.R. or in submarines. In that sense, missiles in Cuba add to an already clear and present danger—although, it should be noted, the nations of Latin America have never previously been subjected to a potential nuclear threat.

But this secret, swift and extraordinary build-up of Communist missiles—in an area well-known to have a special and historical relationship to the United States and the nations of the Western hemisphere, in violation of Soviet assurances, and in defiance of American and hemispheric policy—this sudden, clandestine decision to station strategic weapons for the first time outside of Soviet soil—is a deliberately provocative and unjustified change in the status quo which cannot be accepted by this country, if our courage and our commitments are ever to be trusted again by either friend or foe.

The 1930's taught us a clear lesson: aggressive conduct, if allowed to grow unchecked and unchallenged, ultimately leads to war. This nation is opposed to war. We are also true to our word. Our unswerving objective, therefore, must be to prevent the use of these missiles against this or any other country, and to secure their withdrawal or elimination from the Western hemisphere.

Our policy has been one of patience and restraint, as befits a peaceful and powerful nation which leads a world-wide alliance. We have been determined not to be diverted from our central concerns by mere irritants and fanatics. But now further action is required—and it is underway; and these actions may only be the beginning. We will not prematurely or unnecessarily risk the costs of world-wide nuclear war in which even the fruits of victory would be ashes in our mouth—but neither will we shrink from that risk at any time it must be faced.

Acting, therefore, in the defence of our own security and that of the entire Western hemisphere, and under the authority entrusted to me by the Constitution as endorsed by the resolution of the Congress, I have directed that the following initial steps be taken immediately:

First: To halt this offensive build-up, a strict quarantine on all offensive military equipment under shipment to Cuba is being initiated. All ships of any kind bound for Cuba, from whatever nation or port, will, if found to contain cargoes of offensive weapons, be turned back. This quarantine

will be extended, if needed, to other types of cargo and carriers. We are not at this time, however, denying the necessities of life as the Soviets attempted to do in their Berlin blockade of 1948.

Second: I have directed the continued and increased close surveillance of Cuba and its military build-up. The Foreign Ministers of the O.A.S. in their communiqué of October 6th rejected secrecy on such matters in this hemisphere. Should these offensive military preparations continue, thus increasing the threat to the hemisphere, further action will be justified. I have directed the Armed Forces to prepare for any eventualities; and I trust that, in the interest of both the Cuban people and the Soviet technicians at these sites, the hazards to all concerned of continuing this threat will be recognised.

Third: It shall be the policy of this nation to regard any nuclear missile launched from Cuba against any nation in the Western hemisphere as an attack by the Soviet Union on the United States requiring a full retaliatory response upon the Soviet Union.

Fourth: As a necessary military precaution, I have reinforced our base at Guantanamo, evacuated today the dependents of our personnel there and ordered additional military units to stand by on an alert basis.

Fifth: We are calling tonight for an immediate meeting of the organ of consultation under the Organisation of American States, to consider this threat to hemispheric security and to invoke Articles 6 and 8 of the Rio Treaty in support of all necessary action. The United Nations Charter allows for regional security arrangements—and the nations of this hemisphere decided long ago against the military presence of outside powers. Our other Allies around the world have also been alerted.

Sixth: Under the Charter of the United Nations, we are asking tonight that an emergency meeting of the Security Council be convoked without delay to take action against this latest Soviet threat to world peace. Our resolution will call for the prompt dismantling and withdrawal of all offensive weapons in Cuba, under the supervision of U.N. observers, before the quarantine can be lifted.

Seventh, and finally: I call upon Chairman Khrushchev to halt and eliminate this clandestine, reckless and provocative threat to world peace and to stable relations between our two nations. I call upon him further to abandon this course of world domination, and to join in an historic effort to end the perilous arms race and transform the history of man. He has an opportunity now to move the world back from the abyss of destruction—by returning to his Government's own words that it had no need to station missiles outside its own territory, and withdrawing these weapons from Cuba—by refraining from any action which will widen or deepen the present crisis—and then by participating in a search for peaceful and permanent solutions.

This nation is prepared to present its case against this Soviet threat to peace, and our own proposals for a peaceful world, at any time and in any forum—in the O.A.S., in the United Nations, or in any other meeting that could be useful —without limiting our freedom of action. We have in the past made strenuous efforts to limit the spread of nuclear weapons. We have proposed the elimination of all arms and military bases in a fair and effective disarmament treaty. We are prepared to discuss new proposals for the removal of tensions on both sides—including the possibilities of a genuinely independent Cuba, free to determine its own destiny. We have no wish to war with the Soviet Union—for we are a peaceful people who desire to live in peace with all other peoples.

But it is difficult to settle or even discuss these problems in an atmosphere of intimidation. That is why this latest Soviet threat—or any other threat which is made either independently or in response to our actions this week—must and will be met with determination. Any hostile move anywhere in the world against the safety and freedom of peoples to whom we are committed—including in particular the brave people of West Berlin—will be met by whatever action is needed.

Finally, I want to say a few words to the captive people of Cuba, to whom this speech is being directly carried by special radio facilities. I speak to you as a friend, as one who knows of your deep attachment to your fatherland, as one who shares your aspirations for liberty and justice for all. And I have watched with deep sorrow how your nationalist revolution was betrayed and how your fatherland fell under foreign domination. Now your leaders are no longer Cuban leaders inspired by Cuban ideals. They are puppets and agents of an international conspiracy which has turned Cuba against your friends and neighbours in the Americas—and turned it into the first Latin American country to become a target for nuclear war—the first Latin American country to have these weapons on its soil.

These new weapons are not in your interest. They contribute nothing to your peace and well-being. They can only undermine it. But this country has no wish to cause you to suffer or to impose any system upon you. We know your lives and land are being used as pawns by those who deny your freedom.

Many times in the past, the Cuban people have risen to throw out tyrants who destroyed their liberty. And I have no doubt that most Cubans today look forward to the time when they will be truly free—free from foreign domination, free to choose their own leaders, free to select their own system, free to own their own land, free to speak and write and worship without fear or degradation. And then shall Cuba be welcomed back to the society of free nations and to the associations of this hemisphere.

My fellow citizens: let no one doubt that this is a difficult and dangerous effort on which we have set out. No one can foresee precisely what course it will take or what costs or casualties will be incurred. Many months of sacrifice and self-discipline lie ahead—months in which both our will and our patience will be tested—months in which many threats and denunciations will keep us aware of our danger. But the greatest danger of all would be to do nothing.

The path we have chosen for the present is full of hazards, as all paths are—but it is the one most consistent with our character and courage as a nation and our commitments around the world. The cost of freedom is always high—but Americans have always paid it. And one path we shall never choose is the path of surrender or submission.

Our goal is not the victory of might but the vindication of right, not peace at the expense of freedom, but both peace and freedom, here in this hemisphere, and, we hope, around the world. God willing, that goal will be achieved.

FROM PRESIDENT KENNEDY'S SPEECH PREPARED FOR DELIVERY IN DALLAS, TEXAS

November 22nd, 1963

I want to discuss with you today the status of our strength and our security. This nation's strength and security are not easily or cheaply obtained—nor are they quickly and simply explained. There are many kinds of strength and no one kind will suffice. Overwhelming nuclear strength cannot stop a guerrilla war. Formal pacts of alliance cannot stop internal subversion.

I realise that this nation often tends to identify turning points in world affairs with the major addresses which preceded them. But it was not the Monroe Doctrine that kept all Europe away from this hemisphere—it was the strength of the British Fleet and the width of the Atlantic Ocean. It was not General Marshall's speech at Harvard which kept Communism out of Western Europe—it was the strength and stability made possible by our military and economic assistance.

In this Administration also it has been necessary at times to issue specific warnings—warnings that we could not stand by and watch the Communists conquer Laos by force, or intervene in the Congo, or swallow West Berlin, or maintain offensive missiles in Cuba. But while our goals were at least temporarily obtained in these and other instances, our successful defence of freedom was due—not to the words we used—but to the strength we stood ready to use on behalf of the principles we stand ready to defend.

This strength is composed of many different elements, ranging from the most massive deterrents to the most subtle influence. And all types of strength are needed—no one kind could do the job alone. Let us take a moment, therefore, to review this nation's progress in each major area of strength.

First, the strategic nuclear power of the United States has been so greatly modernised and expanded in the last 1000 days, by the rapid production and deployment of the most modern missile systems, that any and all potential aggressors are clearly confronted now with the impossibility of strategic victory—and the certainty of total destruction—if by reckless attack they should ever force upon us the necessity of a strategic reply.

In less than three years, we have increased by 50 per cent the number of Polaris submarines scheduled to be in force by the next fiscal year—increased by more than 70 per cent our total Polaris purchase programme—increased by more than 75 per cent our Minuteman purchase programme—increased by 50 per cent the portion of our strategic bombers on 15-minute alert—and increased by 100 per cent the total number of nuclear weapons available in our strategic alert forces. Our security is further enhanced by the steps we have taken regarding these weapons to improve the speed and certainty of their response, their readiness at all times to respond, their ability to survive an attack and their ability to be carefully controlled and directed through secure command operations.

But the lessons of the last decade have taught us that freedom cannot be defended by strategic nuclear power alone. We have, therefore, in the last three years accelerated the development and deployment of tactical nuclear weapons—and increased by 60 per cent the tactical nuclear forces deployed in Western Europe.

Nor can Europe or any other continent rely on nuclear forces alone, whether they are strategic or tactical. We have radically improved the readiness of our conventional forces—increased by 45 per cent the number of combat ready army divisions—increased by 100 per cent the procurement of modern army weapons and equipment— increased by 100 per cent our ship construction, conversion and modernisation programme—increased by 100 per cent our procurement of tactical aircraft—increased by 30 per cent the number of tactical air squadrons—and increased the strength of the Marines. As last month's "operation Big Lift"—which originated here in Texas—showed so clearly, this nation is prepared as never before to move substantial numbers of men in surprisingly little time to advanced positions anywhere in the world. We have increased by 175 per cent the procurement of airlift aircraft— and we have already achieved a 75 per cent increase in our existing strategic airlift capability. Finally, moving beyond the traditional roles of our military forces, we have achieved an increase of nearly 600 per cent in our special forces— those forces that are prepared to work with our Allies and friends against the guerrillas, saboteurs, insurgents and assassins who threaten freedom in a less direct but equally dangerous manner.

But American military might should not and need not stand alone against the ambitions of international Communism. Our security and strength, in the last analysis, directly depend on the security and strength of others—and that is why our military and economic assistance plays such a key role in enabling those who live on the periphery of the Communist world to maintain their independence of choice. Our assistance to these nations can be painful, risky and costly—as is true in South-East Asia today. But we dare not weary of the task. For our assistance makes possible the stationing of 3.5 million Allied troops along the Communist frontier at one-tenth the cost of maintaining a comparable number of American soldiers.

About 70 per cent of our military assistance goes to nine key countries located on or near the borders of the Communist bloc—nine countries confronted directly or indirectly with the threat of Communist aggression—Vietnam, Free China, Korea, India, Pakistan, Thailand, Greece, Turkey and Iran. No one of these countries possesses on its own the resources to maintain the forces which our own Chiefs-of-Staff think needed in the common interest. Reducing our efforts to train, equip and assist their armies can only encourage Communist penetration and require in time the increased overseas deployment of American combat forces. And reducing the economic help needed to bolster these nations that undertake to help defend freedom can have the same disastrous result. In short, the $50 billion we spend each year on our own defence could well be ineffective without the $4 billion required for military and economic assistance.

I have spoken of strength largely in terms of the deterrence and resistance of aggression and attack. But, in today's world, freedom can be lost without a shot being fired, by ballots as well as bullets. The success of our leadership is dependent upon respect for our mission in the world as well as our missiles—on a clearer recognition of the virtues of freedom as well as the evils of tyranny.

And that is also why we have regained the initiative in the exploration of outer space—making an annual effort greater than the combined total of all space activities undertaken during the Fifties—launching more than 130 vehicles into earth orbit—putting into actual operation valuable weather and communications satellites—and making it clear to all that the United States of America has no intention of finishing second in space.

There is no longer any fear in the free world that a Communist lead in space will become a permanent assertion of supremacy and the basis of military superiority. There is no longer any doubt about the strength and skill of American science, American industry, American education and the American free enterprise system. In short, our national space effort represents a great gain in, and a great resource of, our national strength—and both Texas and Texans are contributing greatly to this strength.

Finally, it should be clear by now that a nation can be no stronger abroad than she is at home. Only an America which practices what it preaches about equal rights and social justice will be respected by those whose choice affects our future. Only an America which has fully educated its citizens is fully capable of tackling the complex problems and perceiving the hidden dangers of the world in which we live. And only an America which is growing and prospering economically can sustain the world-wide defences of freedom, while demonstrating to all concerned the opportunities of our system and society.

It is clear, therefore, that we are strengthening our security as well as our economy by our recent record increases in national income and output—by surging ahead of most of Western Europe in the rate of business expansion and the margin of corporate profits—by maintaining a more usable level of prices than almost any of our overseas competitors—and by cutting personal and corporate income taxes by some $11 billion, as I have proposed, to assure this nation of the longest and strongest expansion in our peacetime economic history.

We in this country, in this generation, are—by destiny rather than choice—the watchmen on the walls of world freedom. We ask, therefore, that we may be worthy of our power and responsibility—that we may exercise our strength with wisdom and restraint—and that we may achieve in our time and for all time the ancient vision of "peace on earth, good will toward men." That must always be our goal—and the righteousness of our cause must always underlie our strength. For as was written long ago: "Except the Lord keep the city, the watchman waketh but in vain."

Moments in History

The first major problem to face the Kennedy Administration occurred after only three months. An invasion of Cuba had already been planned under President Eisenhower, backed and organised by various uncoordinated government agencies. The actual invasion was to be carried out by Cuban exiles and was to result in the downfall of Fidel Castro. Kennedy gave the project his half-hearted support, and it failed dismally. But it was the President who had to assume responsibility for the whole ill-fated, futile adventure.

This was quickly followed by a European crisis. Despite warnings to Moscow to refrain from any form of unilateral action in Berlin, East Berlin was cut off from the Western sector by the wall on August 13th, 1961. As this development was entirely unexpected, and because it did not appear to affect the essential interests of the United States (the freedom of West Berlin, free access to the city, and the presence there of allied troops), Kennedy decided not to oppose the move. Confidence in American intentions sank to a low ebb, and it is no exaggeration to say that doubts were not allayed until Kennedy's subsequent triumphant visit to Berlin. October 1962 brought the most serious crisis of all, however, when the Soviet Union was discovered to have built bases in Cuba for the launching of intermediate ballistic missiles—a potential threat to the United States. This time the response was immediate and unambiguous—the imposing of a blockade to prevent the further transportation of offensive weapons to Cuba. The Soviet Union was forced to beat a retreat. Kennedy had proved that his policy of combining firmness with flexibility in difficult situations had stood the test.

President Kennedy made certain that during his whole period in office contact was maintained with the Soviet Union by means of conversational exchanges. This he felt was imperative in view of the continually shifting balance of power in the field of strategic deterrence, his own personal responsibility for preserving world peace and the avoidance of an accidental nuclear holocaust. In the spring of 1963, the opportunity came to reach a partial solution of this most vital of all problems. On August 5th, 1963, an agreement was concluded in Moscow between the United States, the Soviet Union and the United Kingdom, banning nuclear tests in the air, in outer space and under water. Kennedy considered it—and so it appeared to the world at large—a first step towards solving further outstanding issues in this field. In November 1963, it seemed to Kennedy that the time had come—taking into account the 1964 election campaign—to secure his following in certain key States by making public appearances. The most difficult, but potentially the most rewarding area was the South. After a cool reception at the outset of his tour in Florida and then at Fort Worth, Texas, the political climate had visibly improved by the time he reached Dallas. Tens of thousands of people lined the streets to greet the President. At the height of this unexpected and encouraging reception, the bullets of assassin Lee Harvey Oswald struck the President. It was November 22nd, 1963, and the time of his death one hour after noon.

I bear the responsibility o
the Presidency of the Unite
States, and it is my duty to
make decisions that no advise
and no Ally can make for me

Cuba

October 1962 brought the most serious political crisis in President Kenne dy's term of office when it was discovered that the Soviet Union had secretl begun to install rocket bases in Cuba. Kennedy reacted swiftly and firmly wit the announcement of a blockade. With world tension at its highest point i years, notes flew back and forth between Moscow and Washington. Finally th Soviet Union agreed to withdraw their rockets and the world stepped bac from the brink of war.

Right: The unloading of rockets in the harbour at Mariel and the setting u of rocket bases in the interior of the island was discovered and photographe by American reconnaissance planes.

Below: During the blockade a Russian submarine cruised in the Caribbea The Soviet flag with the red star can be seen clearly.

On Monday evening, October 22nd, 1962, President Kennedy addressed the American public on a nationwide television network and announced that rocket bases had been established in Cuba. He issued a solemn warning that the launching of any rocket from these bases toward any country would be taken as an act of war against the United States. On the following day the President signed an executive order forbidding the import of offensive weapons into Cuba and blockading the island. It came into force at 2 p.m. on October 24th.

During the critical period the American military stood alert. Guantanamo; the U.S. base on Cuba, was heavily reinforced and

substantial troops were quartered near the coast of Florida, ready for an attack on Cuba. The U.S. Navy concentrated more than 100 units in the seas off Cuba for blockade duty and to act in any emergency.

The firm actions of the U.S. and allied nations was successful in persuading the Soviet Union to withdraw the majority of the rockets. On November 7th, 1962, the Russian freighter "Fizik Kurchatov" left Cuba with six medium range rockets on board. Other ships carried the remaining rockets back to Russia. Instead of self-congratulations, Kennedy praised Premier Khrushchev's desire to keep the peace.

Berlin

*Freedom is indivisible. And when one man is enslaved,
all are not free. When all are free, then we can look
forward to that day when this city will be joined as one—
and this country and this great continent of Europe—
in a peaceful and hopeful globe.*

*When that day finally comes—as it will—the people of
West Berlin can take sober satisfaction in the fact
that they were in the front lines for almost two decades.*

Right: In February 1962, the brother of the President, Attorney General Robert F. Kennedy, visited Berlin and brought greetings from the President to Willy Brandt. On his arrival Robert Kennedy paid a visit to the wall near Potsdamer Platz.

We cannot and will not permit the Communists to drive us out of Berlin, either gradually or by force. For the fulfillment of our pledge to that city is essential to the morale and security of West Germany, to the unity of western Europe, and to the faith of the entire free world.

On June 26th, 1963, towards the close of his visit to Germany, President Kennedy went to West Berlin where a great reception awaited him. With Lord Mayor Willy Brandt and Chancellor Konrad Adenauer he was driven through the city.

More than a million people in West Berlin packed the streets to greet President Kennedy on his drive through the city. And over 250,000 of them heard the famous speech on the square in front of the Schöneberger Rathaus.

All free men, wherever they may be,
re citizens of Berlin. Therefore, as a free man,
take pride in the words: "Ich bin ein
Berliner."

There are many people in the world who really don't understand—or say they don't—what is the great issue between the free world and the Communist world. Let them come to Berlin.

There are some who say that Communism is the wave of the future. Let them come to Berlin.
And there are some who say—in Europe and elsewhere—we can work with the Communists. Let them come to Berlin.

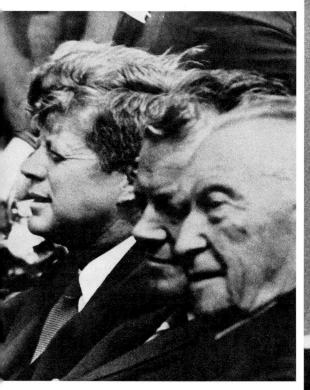

The wall is the most obvious and vivid demonstration of the failures of the Communist system. For it is an offence not only against history, but an offence against humanity.

Our problems are man-made—therefore, they can be solved by man. And man can be as big as he wants. No problem of human destiny is beyond the reach of human beings. Man's reason and spirit have often solved the seemingly unsolvable—and we believe they can do it again.

All this will not be finished in the first one hundred days. Nor will it be finished in the first one thousand days, nor in the life of this Administration, nor even perhaps in our lifetime on this planet. But let us begin.

THE LAST DAY

On the morning of his last day of life, he arose early, left his Fort Worth hotel, walked with buoyant stride through a slight mist to a nearby parking lot, where several thousand Texans were waiting behind barricades to see him. Explaining why Jackie had not accompanied him, the President laughed. "Mrs. Kennedy", he said, "is busy organizing herself. It takes a little longer, you know, but then she looks so much better than we do." And indeed she looked lovely when, wearing a pink wool suit and pillbox hat, she joined her husband at a breakfast sponsored by the Fort Worth Chamber of Commerce.

Next on the President's schedule was Dallas, and during the flight there he put the finishing touches on a speech he meant to deliver at noon. Its concluding words: "We in this country, in this generation, are—by destiny rather than choice—the watchmen on the walls of world freedom. We ask therefore that we may be worthy of our power and responsibility—that we may exercise our strength with wisdom and restraint—and that we may achieve in our time and for all time the ancient vision of 'peace on earth, good will toward men.' That must always be our goal—and the righteousness of our cause, must always underlie our strength. For, as was written long ago: 'Except the Lord keep the city, the watchman waketh but in vain.'"

At the Dallas airport, nearly 5,000 people were waiting. The President, in a dark blue suit, stepped from his plane smiling happily. He and Jackie were met by a committee that gave her a bouquet of red roses. Their car was ready to leave, but Kennedy had to shake hands with some voters. Jackie, her roses cradled in her left arm, also touched the outstretched hands. After a few minutes she started to walk away, but, noticing that her husband was still at it, smiled fondly, said "There he goes", and returned.

Finally, at 11.50 a.m. C.S.T., they entered the presidential limousine and began to drive into Dallas.

THE ASSASSINATION

To President Kennedy, popularity was the breath of life—and now he was breathing of it deeply. Texas was supposed to be a hostile political land, but for 23 hours he had been acclaimed there. Conservative Dallas was supposed to be downright dangerous, but he had just come from a warm airport welcome and along much of his motorcade route in the downtown district he had basked in waves of applause from crowds lined ten and twelve deep. What was about to happen must have been the farthest thing from his mind.

Next to him sat Jackie. In front of them, on jump seats of the President's Lincoln, its bubbletop off, were Texas' Democratic Governor John Connally, 46, and his wife Nellie. As the President's car approached an underpass near the intersection of Elm, Main and Commerce Streets, Nellie Connally turned to Kennedy, said laughingly: "You can't say that Dallas isn't friendly to you today." The President started to reply. . . .

That reply was stilled by a shot. It was 12.30 p.m. C.S.T. and in a split second a thousand things happened. The President's body slumped to the left; his right leg shot up over the car door. A woman close by at the curb saw it. "My God!" she screamed. "He's shot!" Blood gushed from the President's head as it came to rest in Jackie's lap. "Jack!" she cried. "Oh, no! No!"

John Connally turned—and by turning, probably saved his own life. There were two more shots, and a bullet pierced his back, plowed down through his chest, fractured his right wrist, and lodged in his left thigh. A photographer looked up at a seven-story building on the corner—the Texas School Book Depository, a warehouse for textbooks—and caught a glimpse of a rifle barrel being withdrawn from a window on the sixth floor.

There was a shocked, momentary stillness, a frozen tableau. Then Kennedy's driver cried: "Let's get out of here quick!" He automatically pulled out of the motorcade—the set procedure in emergencies. The Secret Service agent next to him grabbed the radio telephone, called ahead to the police escorts, and ordered them to make for the nearest hospital. Jackie bent low, cradling the President's head in her lap, and the Lincoln bolted ahead as if the shots themselves had gunned the engine into life. Spurting to 70 m.p.h., it fled down the highway, rounding curves on two wheels. A Secret Service man, who had jumped onto the rear bumper of the car, flung himself across the trunk, and in his anger and frustration pounded it repeatedly with his fist.

Dallas

Below: At noon on November 22nd, 1963, President John F. Kennedy and his wife arrived at Dallas Airport, Texas. They were received by Governor John Connally of Texas.

Following double page: President Kennedy and his wife Jacqueline, the Governor of Texas, John Connally and his wife Nellie, on their way through Dallas, shortly before the attempt on their lives.

When they killed him in his pity,
When they killed him in his prime . . .
. . . They killed him in his kindness,
In their madness, in their blindness,
And they killed him from behind . . .

HERMAN MELVILLE

The mortal remains of the murdered President lie in state inside the Capitol. Members of all the Armed Forces stand guard around the coffin.

Jacqueline Kennedy, displaying remarkable self-control, leaves the Capitol, hand-in-hand with her children.

The President's funeral procession on its way to the Arlington National Cemetery. In the background is the Lincoln Memorial.

Below: President Kennedy's last journey across Arlington National Cemetery.

Right: After the interment of her husband an officer of the U.S. Army hands the President's widow the folded flag of the United States. Next to Jacqueline Kennedy is her brother-in-law, Robert Kennedy.

Following double-page: Never before in history has the burial of a statesman brought together so many reigning monarchs and heads of State. First row from left to right: President Lübke of Western Germany, General de Gaulle, Queen Frederika of Greece, King Baudouin of Belgium, Emperor Haile Selassie of Ethiopia, and President Chunghee Pak of South Korea.

MURDER MOST FOUL

The first need of the country is to take to heart the nature of this unspeakable crime. There is no public crisis at home or abroad which demands such instant attention that it cannot wait until we have collected ourselves and can proceed deliberately. But there is a searing internal crisis within the American spirit which we have first to realize and then to resolve.

The American future depends on it, and our capacity to govern ourselves. What we have to realize is that, though speech and gossip and rumour are free, the safety of the Republic is at stake when extremists go unrestrained. Extremists may profess any ideology. But what they all have in common is that they treat opponents as enemies, outside the laws and the community of their fellow men.

What happened in Dallas could, to be sure, have happened in another city. But it must be said that the murder of the President was not the first act of political violence in that city, but one in a series. The man who is now the President of the United States was manhandled by his fellow Texans. The man who represents the United States at the United Nations was spat upon.

In this atmosphere of political violence lived the President's murderer, himself addicted to the fascination of violence in his futile and lonely and brooding existence. The salient fact about him was his alienation from humanity, from country, family and friends. Nothing within him, it would seem, bound him to the President or to the Governor as human beings. No human feeling stayed his hand.

In his alienation Oswald turned to the left. But that was incidental. Those who spat on Mr. Johnson and on Mr. Stevenson had turned to the right. The common characteristic of all of them was their alienation, the loss of their ties, the rupture of the community.

An extremist is an outsider. For him the government in Washington is a hated foreign power and the President in Washington is an invading conqueror. There is no limit, therefore, to his hatred, which feeds upon the venom of malice, slander, and hallucination.

In Dallas today there is much search of conscience, and well there should be. For Dallas has long been conspicuous for its tolerance of extremists, and for the inability of its decent citizens, undoubtedly the great majority, to restrain the extremists and restore a condition of honest and temperate and reasonable discussion.

It was comforting, therefore, to read on Sunday that the mayor of Dallas, Earle Cabell, had said that 'each of us, in prayerful reflection, must search his heart and determine if, through intemperate word or deed, we might have contributed in some fashion to the movement of this mind across the brink of insanity.'

We must all follow the mayor of Dallas in that prayerful reflection. For it is only too easy to forget that in a free country there must be not only liberty and equality but also fraternity.

The only solace for the nation's shame and grief can come from a purge, or at least the reduction of, the hatred and venom which lie so close to the surface of our national life. We have allowed the community of the American people to be rent with enmity. Only if and as we can find our way back into the American community will we find our way back to confidence in the American destiny.

We must stop the flow of the poison that when men differ, say about taxes or civil rights, or Russia, they cannot be reconciled by persuasion and debate, and that those who take the other view are implacable enemies. In the light of this monstrous crime, we can see that in a free country, which we are and intend to be, unrestrained speech and thought are inherently subversive. Democracy can be made to work only when the bonds of the community are inviolate, and stronger than all the parties and factions and interests and sects.

I wish I felt certain that the self-realization into which grief has shocked us will endure when we go back about our business. The divisive force of hatred and ungovernability are strong among us, and the habit of intemperate speech and thought has become deeply ingrained.

It is deepened by the strains of war and the frustrations of this revolutionary age, by the exploitation of violence and cruelty in the mass media, by the profusion of weapons and by the presence of so many who know how to use them.

But I do have much hope in the healing art of Lyndon Johnson. We can turn to him with confidence. For his great gift is in finding the consensus without which the American system of government, with its states and regions, its checks and balances, is unworkable.

To find the consensus among our divided and angry people is his historic opportunity. To restore the internal peace of the United States is his unique mission.

That done, all else will be manageable. WALTER LIPPMANN

The greatest leader of our time has been struck down by the foulest deed of our time. Today John Fitzgerald Kennedy lives on in the immortal words and works that he left behind. He lives on in the mind and memories of mankind. He lives on in the hearts of his countrymen.

No words are sad enough to express our sense of loss. No words are strong enough to express our determination to continue the forward thrust of America that he began.

The dream of conquering the vastness of space—the dream of partnership across the Atlantic—and across the Pacific as well—the dream of a Peace Corps in less developed nations—the dream of education for all of our children—the dream of jobs for all who seek them and need them—the dream of care for our elderly—the dream of an all-out attack on mental illness—and above all, the dream of equal rights for all Americans, whatever their race or color—these and other American dreams have been vitalized by his drive and by his dedication.

And now the ideas and ideals which he so nobly represented must and will be translated into effective action.

LYNDON B. JOHNSON
PRESIDENT OF THE UNITED STATES OF AMERICA

PICTURE CREDITS

Ambassade Francaise 91
ASL 75, 105, 106
Associated Press 175
ATP 26, 29
Berliner Senat 162, 164
Bildzeitung 166
British Information Service 101
Bundesbildstelle, Bonn 107, 109, 110, 111, 112, 164
Cornell Capa, Magnum 29, 41, 70, 155
Diamant 78, 79
Dukas 23, 26, 29, 72, 77, 80, 87, 132, 140, 154, 160
Fischer 65
Bob Henriques, Magnum 120
Keystone 27, 103, 106, 118, 159, 161, 165
Krüger 47
Jung 161, 164, 168
Gus Manos, Magnum 67, 69
Match 46, 50, 93
Mondadori Press 172

Photopress 71, 72, 73, 74, 129
Ringier-Bild 171, 176, 184
Dennis Stock, Magnum 68
Tièche 48
Tikhomiroff, Magnum 80
Ullstein Bilderdienst 73, 136
United States Information Service (USIS) 18, 20, 21, 22, 23, 24, 25, 26, 27, 30, 31, 32, 42, 43, 44, 45, 46, 48, 49, 50, 51, 52, 53, 54, 55, 76, 77, 79, 89, 90, 92, 94, 97, 99, 102, 104, 108, 113, 114, 115, 116, 117, 119, 120, 129, 130, 131, 133, 134, 136, 137, 138, 139, 141, 142, 143, 144, 153, 154, 155, 156, 157, 163, 165, 178, 179, 180, 181, 182, 183
Votava 95, 96, 98

Cover: USIS
Back cover: Cornell Capa, Magnum

Text by Walter Lippmann on pages 187
Copyright © 1964 by Cosmopress, Geneva